Wild Women
IN THE KITCHEN

Wild Women

IN THE KITCHEN

101 Rambunctious Recipes & 99 Tasty Tales

The Wild Women Association

Foreword & Recipes by
Nicole Alper with Lynette Rohrer of Star*s

Introduction by Autumn Stephens

CONARI PRESS
Berkeley, California

Conari Press books are distributed by Publishers Group West

Cover Design: Brenda Duke, Suzanne Albertson
Interior Design: Suzanne Albertson
Cover photo: Kelly Povo, Minneapolis, MN

ISBN: 1-57324-030-3

Acknowledgment of permission to reprint previously published material can be
found on page 227, which constitutes an extension of the copyright page.

Kind permission was granted by Archive Photo for reproduction of all
interior images with the exception of those on pages 10 and 37.

Images of "Betty Crocker" are reprinted with the generous
permission of General Mills, Inc.

Library of Congress Cataloging-in-Publication Data

Wild women in the kitchen: 101 rambunctious recipes and 99 tasty tales / the Wild Women
Association; introduction by Autumn Stephens; foreword by Nicole Alper.

p.   cm.
Includes bibliographical references and index.
ISBN 1-57324-030-3 (trade paper)
1. Cookery.   2. Women—Anecdotes.
3. Celebrities.   I. Wild Women Association.
TX714.W522   1996
641.5—dc20   96-4937

Printed in the United States of America on recycled paper

10   9   8   7   6   5   4

- Acknowledgments -

This book was born through the labor of many wild women, including:

Brenda Knight, the generation of the idea and marketing

Vicki León, research

Lynette Rohrer and *Nicole Alper,* recipe testing and
donation of original recipes

Autumn Stephens, inspiration and introduction

Barbara Quick, stories and recipes from M.F.K. Fisher and Jessica Mitford

Joan Hemm and *The Shady Ladies of the Central City Motherlode,* quotes

Claudia Schaab, research

Emily Miles, research and publicity

Ame Beanland, research, design, and production

Amity Stauffer, typing

Chandrika Madhavan, typing

Eileen Swanson, typing

Susan Stafford, research

Suzanne Albertson, interior design, layout, and cover design

Erin McCune, publicity

Barbara Parmet, recipe

Marie-Jeanne and *Dominique Delanghe,* croissant recipe

Diane Clement of *The Tomato Fresh Food Cafe,* recipes

Brenda Duke, cover design

Judy July and *Generic Type,* cover work

M. J. Ryan, research, recipes, and editing

Cooking Something Up Together

Women of all generations and ages have shared one very special and constant lover—food. This sweet-talking seducer lures women out of bed for many a late-night rendezvous, causing us to bask in the unforgiving light of the refrigerator as we eagerly devour leftovers. This tempter offers itself in ever-changing and enthusiastic forms—the sensuousness of a chocolate torte, the boldness of a ripe strawberry, or the inventiveness of a white corn soufflé—and, through its metamorphosis, succeeds in keeping us faithful, our affections unwavering, even sometimes bordering on obsession.

My obsession began very early. My mother Jeanne-Berenice is French, and though she was orphaned in World War II and never had anyone to teach her how to cook, one could say she was genetically predisposed to being a great chef. The scent of Boeuf Bourguignonne would waft through our house on a regular basis. When other children were bringing bologna sandwiches to school, my mother supplied me with a Tupperware container of Coq au Vin and a slice of Quatre Quart (a French pound cake, the recipe for which you will find later in the book).

I suppose the cooking gene was passed on, and in my early twenties, I temporarily left school to pursue my interest in cooking. I went to the California Culinary Academy in San Francisco, where I had the distinct pleasure of meeting Lynette Rohrer, now the Executive Pastry Chef of Star's, in Palo Alto. Though Lynette never finished the Academy, she went on to work in the most distinguished restaurants in the San Francisco Bay Area: Postrio, Chez Panisse, Bisou, Masa's, and now Star's. We lived together during cooking school, and my fondest memory of Lynette displaying her skills was when she, during a fairly wild party, approached me and several friends in the hot tub to offer up a fine display of caramelized Spam triangles, elegantly nestled in a silver serving dish.

That is undoubtedly a charming quality in a chef: though one's skills in the kitchen may be extraordinary, there is no reason to be a food snob. In fact, one evening she and I were dining at Masa's (her employee discount made the meal only exorbitantly, not unconscionably, expensive), and after a meal that could only be described as a religious experience, dessert arrived. The chef, knowing Lynette's predilection for junk food, put together a phenomenal array of twinkies sliced on the bias, ho-ho's swimming in crème anglaise, red zingers resting on a pool of red raspberry puree, all beautifully garnished with a brunoise of red and black licorice, gracefully scattered on the plate. She eagerly gobbled it up.

Until all too recently women's love affair with food was considered illicit if it dared to cross the boundary into the professional kitchen. Thanks to many dedicated wild women, our gender now openly displays and profits from this liaison. From being head chefs in some of the finest restaurants, to hosting and producing gourmet cooking shows, to even the tyrannical homemaking of Martha Stewart, women have dared to take what we were once expected to do at home, and turn these daily tasks of food preparation into an extraordinary and often lucrative art form.

Wild Women in the Kitchen looks at some of these pioneers, as well as at women who were trendsetters in food fads and food production, and those who were famous gourmands. It takes you on a journey, an unpredictable exploration, of famous women and their relationships to food. Some have made a life of cooking; others (of different notoriety) simply have an unexpected favorite recipe. What they all have in common is a fervent love of food.

Wild Women in the Kitchen offers recipes that can service the gourmet and the scavenger; elegant foods that require preparation and thought, and others that can satisfy an instant hunger. You can host a romantic dinner for two with a Passion Fruit Lobster Appetizer, Artichoke Heart Timbale, and Chocolate Fondue, or you can gather a group of friends for a night of Penne Pesto Pasta Salad and home-brewed beer.

Lynette and I have enjoyed testing and contributing recipes for this one-of-a kind cookbook and hope you will find it enjoyable too. And in the words of a very well-known wild gourmet who really liked her sherry, "Bon Appetit!"

—Nicole Alper

A Taste of Things to Come

There are strong women who can be moved to tears by the burnished purple beauty of an eggplant, the subtle upward arc of a banana, as promising as a new moon or a smile. There are plain-living women who believe that there is poetry in mashed potatoes, yet would sooner eat their old-fashioned argyles than a forkful of arugula. There are iron-willed women who revel in secret fantasies about that proverbial pie in the sky, the kind that exerts no gravitational pull on the hips. There are sunny-side-up women who make tequila sunrises when life gives them lemons. There are down-to-earth women who never forget to count their blessings—or to ask for second helpings. Tastes vary; what is universal is the primal pleasure we take in feeding our faces—and in the process, our souls.

For most of us, our introduction to inspirational dining was also our introduction to dining, period. A heady mixture of Mom—our own private Omnipotent Goddess/Feeding Machine—and warm milk, that punchy post-natal nosh sparked not only our passion for consuming, but our consuming passion for the most fascinating woman in our lives.

Eventually, of course, our interests expanded to include activities (earning a living, for example) other than chowing down and gazing adoringly at our parental unit. Yet according to a rather robust, apple-cheeked painter I once knew, we hedonistic human beings actually dreamed up the adult diversions of art, literature, and music only because we couldn't spend every waking moment eating or making love. (Between meals of one sort or another, Ms. Freud liked to dabble in watercolors.)

I suspect, however, that something both more and less substantial than either the mechanics of the human body (which, contrary to the impression one might pick up from the current crop of fashion magazines, really does require the regular consumption of food) or the infantile whims of the id, that hollow-legged, bottomless pit of the psyche, drives us to eat and drink. True, the ascetic Joan of Arc, as we learn later in these pages, liked to get a little bombed before doing battle: under duress, France's famous virgin warrior would dunk a chunk of broth-soaked bread in a cup of wine and call it dinner. (Today, we call it French onion soup.) And even the decorous afternoon tea—that most restrained and ritualized of meals—was the brainchild of a lady with an appetite too lusty to tolerate the wait for a fashionably late dinner.

Yet as savvy take-out queens, mavens of fine cuisine, and the chef at your neighborhood bistro all know, the contemplation and consumption of certain foods often transcends purely physiological ends, becoming an aesthetic experience in its own right, the gustatory equivalent of ogling a luscious Renoir, or sighing over a sonnet by Shakespeare, or slow-dancing with an old beau, in some deliciously world-weary boîte , to a torch singer's bittersweet song.

For our favorite feminist fatales throughout history—women whose lives were as quirky and quixotic as their tastes in food—an intriguing variety of comestibles helped induce a sublime mood. The divine dancer Josephine Baker, as you are about to read, found that a bit of bubbly rocked her socks (at least on those occasions when she was clad in something more than a G-string). Her own hors d'oeuvres turned the trick for the scandalous salon-keeper Natalie Barney, known, in the early 1900s, for making a mean cucumber sandwich, and also a famous French courtesan. Avant-garde art-lover Alice B. Toklas turned on with her psychotropic fudge; in the mind of Catherine the Great, large quantities of caviar were the key to successful copulation. And in twentieth-century America, a whole host of modern-day Mary Poppinses—among them Frieda Caplan, who transformed her fondness for fruit into a multimillion dollar industry—still find nothing so festive as a tea party on the glass ceiling.

In life as in the kitchen, of course, there are no surefire formulas for wild success (although Frida Kahlo's Chicken Escabeche looks like a winner to me). For connoisseurs of good food and great women, however, this eclectic volume offers a soul-satisfying smorgasbord of recipes, remembrances, and truly obscure trivia (including, incidentally, the biologically sound reason why women actually need their chocolate). Follow the recipes, if you will, with pleasure; consume with passion.

—Autumn Stephens, author of *Wild Women*
and *Wild Words from Wild Women*

Alluring Appetizers

The Liberated Danseuse

Isadora Duncan, who revolutionized the dance world in the late 1800s with her spontaneous, flowing style that released the art form from the constraints of classical ballet—was equally free-form in her personal life. She wore loose, flowing gowns while she danced, baring her legs and breasts, shocking stuffy Victorians in Europe and the United States, and setting a trend that would eventually liberate women from corsets and stays. A firm disbeliever in marriage—although she did eventually tie the knot, at age forty-one, with a Russian poet seventeen years her junior—she had two children out of wedlock and many lovers. She also had one of the most dramatic deaths in history. In 1927, at the age of forty-nine, she was strangled to death by her own scarf when it became entangled in the rear wheel of a Bugatti sports car. She was not driving, she was being chauffeured by a car salesman with whom she had become illicitly involved.

As might be expected in one who lived and died so flamboyantly, Isadora had an extravagant palate, often craving the most rare and expensive of foods—asparagus, strawberries, champagne, and caviar. Since she was not able to afford such fare, friends often prepared her favorite delicacies for her, rescuing Isadora from the fate of conventional cuisine.

Asparagus Salad

1 pound asparagus

2 tablespoons red wine vinegar

6 tablespoons extra-virgin olive oil

1 teaspoon Dijon-style mustard

1 tablespoon chopped capers

2 teaspoons minced shallots

4 tablespoons chopped fresh parsley

Salt and pepper to taste

Prepare the asparagus by snapping off the woody ends wherever they naturally break when you apply pressure, and place in a steamer basket. Place in a pan large enough for the asparagus to lie flat, cover, and steam on high for 5 to 10 minutes depending on thickness of spears. Asparagus is done when a sharp knife easily pierces the root end. Submerge the asparagus in an ice bath to stop the cooking and place on to a towel to drain. Refrigerate until cold.

Meanwhile, combine remaining ingredients in a small mixing bowl with a fork or wire whisk. Arrange cold asparagus on serving dish and drizzle the vinaigrette on top. Serves 4.

"Asparagus should be sexy and almost fluid..."
—Diana Vreeland

That's Not Potatoes in Your Basket

The Biblical **Judith** was a very beautiful and stubborn widow who lived in the town of Bethulia and saved her city in the face of total destruction. Enemy troops, led by General Holofernes, rapidly approached the tranquil town and managed to cut off its water supply. The elders, wracked with fear and a sense of hopelessness, had the audacity to give God an ultimatum: let it rain for five days, or they will surrender.

Judith, being the cunning woman she was, set out with a basket of rich cheeses and a jug of wine to meet the general. Already intoxicated by her beauty, and driven to consume the wine because of the cheese, Holofernes was soon snoozing like a new-born babe. Upon which Judith grabbed his sword from its sheath, adeptly sliced off the great leader's head, and carefully tucked it into her basket. When his troops approached the following day, they found

their leader's head mounted on a stake outside the city gate, and ran in horror. In honor of Judith, Jewish people incorporate cheese into the menu on the holy day of Chanukah.

Potato latkes, eaten in countless Jewish American households, are actually an adaptation of Sephardic cheese latkes. Because not many European Jews had ready access to cheese, they substituted something they had plenty of—potatoes. We have suggested a fruit compote to accompany the pancakes. It, too, is a traditional Chanukah food.

Potato Latkes with Apple and Pear Compote

(Nicole Alper)

Compote

1 tablespoon granulated sugar

1 tablespoon vanilla extract

½ cup Calvados

1 large pear (peeled, cored, and sliced)

2 large apples (peeled, cored, and sliced)

1 teaspoon ground cinnamon

2 tablespoons butter

Potato Latkes

3 large potatoes

1 small onion

2 eggs

1 tablespoon flour

1 teaspoon salt

Vegetable oil for frying

Make the compote: Melt the butter in a sauté pan. Sprinkle the fruit with the cinnamon and sugar and sauté in the butter for one minute at a moderately low heat. Deglaze with the Calvados and add the vanilla. Bring to a low simmer and continue cooking for 3 to 4 minutes. Remove from heat and let cool a bit while you make the latkes.

Peel and grate potatoes into a mixing bowl. Squeeze out remaining liquid or drain in a colander for a few minutes. Peel and grate the onions into the potatoes. Mix in the eggs and then the flour. Add salt and stir into a smooth batter. Heat oil in frying pan (enough to cover the latkes). Drop a tablespoon of batter (approximately 3″ wide) into the hot oil. When brown, turn and brown on other side. Be careful not to let the oil smoke. When golden on both sides, drain on paper towels.

For a healthier variation: Use the same batter, but pour it into a well-greased muffin pan. Bake at 350 degrees for about 45 minutes or until done and a knife inserted into the center comes out clean. Serves 6 to 8.

Women, Food, and Films

- Home for the Holidays;
- Eating: A Very Serious Comedy About Women & Food;
- The Wedding Banquet;
- Eat, Drink, Man, Woman;
- Breakfast at Tiffany's;
- Tampopo;
- Steel Magnolias;
- Babette's Feast (based on a short story by Isak Dinesen);
- The Cook, the Thief, His Wife, and Her Lover;
- Like Water for Chocolate (also a novel).

Oprah's Favorite Pick-Me-Up
—Then and Now

In Nellie Bly's biography of **Oprah Winfrey**, Bly describes the following incident from the Queen of Daytime TV's heftier days. "Oprah halted taping and shouted to a crewman: 'Get me my Lay's™ potato chips! I don't care what you have to do to get them—just get them now or I won't finish the show!' The man ran out and bought five, fifteen-ounce bags. Oprah ate her fill and then continued taping, proving that you could always count on her when the chips were down."

In recent years, Oprah has cut down on such greasy goodies with the assistance of Rosie Daley, formerly a chef for the Cal-a-Vie spa, whom Oprah calls her "diet cop." With Rosie's help, she dropped fifty-five pounds, and Rosie made the Women's Food Hall of Fame with the bestselling lowfat cookbook, *In the Kitchen with Rosie*. Here we offer some tasty tidbits to honor both the old and new incarnations of Oprah. The homemade potato chips and Tasty Tuna Dip are rich treats, so for those days when you are looking for something lighter, we include a lowfat dip and substitute raw vegetables.

Potato Chips

2 large russet potatoes

Enough vegetable oil to half fill a deep fryer

Salt to taste

Peel and slice the potatoes very thinly with a vegetable peeler, or light pressure on a Cuisinart using the slicer blade. Soak the potato slices in cold water for at least an hour and change the water two or three times: this is the secret to crispy, tasty potato chips. Dry thoroughly by patting with paper towels.

Heat the oil up to 375 degrees (the oil must be extremely hot). If you are using a deep fryer, put only enough potato slices in the basket so that they are not clumped together. Drop the basket into the oil—it will start bubbling. Shake and stir frequently so the chips don't stick together. Cook until golden brown, 1 to 3 minutes. Remove onto paper towels to drain and salt. Serves 4.

(You can also make these in a wok if you have a wire mesh ladle, which in some ways is better because you can toss the slices in one at a time and remove individually when done.)

Dill Dip

1 cup nonfat sour cream

1 cup nonfat mayonnaise

*2 teaspoons dried dill weed or 2 tablespoons
very finely minced fresh dill weed*

2 teaspoons dried parsley or 2 tablespoons
very finely minced fresh parsley

Combine all ingredients in a medium bowl and stir well. Cover and refrigerate at least one hour. Serve with chips or raw vegetables. Will keep in the refrigerator for up to a week. Serves 10.

Tasty Tuna Dip

1 6½ ounce can of tuna packed in water, drained

4 tablespoons butter, softened

1 teaspoon finely grated lemon zest (about one lemon)

2 tablespoons lemon juice

2 tablespoons olive oil

½ teaspoon dried oregano

1 clove garlic, pressed

Pepper to taste

Place all ingredients in a food processor and process until creamy. Transfer to a bowl and serve at room temperature. Serve with breadsticks or raw vegetables. Makes about 1 cup.

"My idea of heaven is a great big baked potato
and someone to share it with."
—Oprah Winfrey

Cleopatra's Pearls

liny the Elder says **Cleopatra** made a bet with Marc Antony that she could spend the equivalent of two million dollars on a single banquet. Cleopatra won the bet when she dissolved her huge pearl earring in a tumbler of very strong vinegar. The pearl was one of the largest in the world and very, very valuable. She was about to dunk the other earring when the referee called a halt, declaring her the winner. Historian Vicki León, author of *Uppity Women of Ancient Times*, claims this is hyperbole—that scientists have subsequently proven that pearls do not dissolve in vinegar. Nonetheless, she admits, the story does stand as a testimony to Cleo's profligate ways and theatricality.

Once you've melted all your pearls, presuming that it is possible, what's left but to eat the oysters? Do as the Very Rich do. Rumor has it that this recipe, adapted from one by Marla Trump—a big spender, but not quite in Cleopatra's league—stimulates more than just an appetite for dinner.

Orgiastic Oysters

20 fresh oysters, shucked and drained

6 tablespoons butter, warmed to room temperature

3 teaspoons fresh ginger

2 tablespoons lime juice

Salt and pepper to taste
¼ bunch cilantro, chopped
⅔ cup bread crumbs

Prepare the oysters by loosening the meat from the shell, draining the juices, and setting each one aside. (The oysters should remain in the shell.)

Meanwhile, melt the butter and sauté the garlic for one minute over low heat. Stir in the ginger, lime juice, salt, and pepper. Set aside.

Blend the bread crumbs and cilantro together and spread over the oysters. Drizzle 1 tablespoon of the butter mixture over each oyster. Broil until the bread crumbs are lightly browned and the oysters are warmed through. Serve immediately. Serves 4.

"You ought to try to eat raw oysters in a restaurant with every
eye focused on you. It makes you feel as if the creatures
were whales, your fork a derrick, and your
mouth the Mammoth Cave."
—Lillian Russell

Beyond Oysters: Other Alluring Aphrodisiacs

*L*iterally hundreds of substances—many of which you really wouldn't want to eat or even read about—are said to be aphrodisiacs. The most famous of these is Spanish fly, a variety of blister beetle (*cantharides*) that has long been associated (at least in the male mind) with the so-called weaker sex. According to Peter James and Nick Thorpe in *Ancient Inventions,* "the Roman empress Livia, scheming wife of Augustus (31 B.C.–A.D. 14), purportedly slipped it into the food of other members of the imperial family to stimulate them into committing sexual indiscretions that could later be used against them."

Another well-known user of Spanish fly was **Catherine Monvoisin,** also known as "La Voisin," a seventeenth-century French apothecary. In January 1680, she was accused of providing love potions and poisons to six important ladies at court. (The reason for the love potions is obvious; the poisons were supplied for the removal of undesirable husbands and rivals of their own sex.) Princess de Tingry, who had asked for love charms that would make her more erotic, was given a severed hand and a toad—presumably to place under her pillow. For the rest, "La Voisin" made a concoction of Spanish fly, henbane, and thorn apple. Her arrest led to an investigation ordered by King Louis XIV that eventually included 442 people, including his favorite mistress, the Marquise de Montespan, who was banished from his affections thereafter. "La Voisin" herself was burned at the stake.

If you are looking to spice up your love life in a more flavorful fashion, among the more appetizing aphrodisiacs are chocolate, shellfish, venison—for

its robust, wild flavor—and caviar. Colette was said to have prized truffles as an aphrodisiac, while Catherine the Great was supposedly not able to conceive a child until she served one of her lovers a vast quantity of caviar before a night of consummate passion.

Here are three recipes sure to stir the embers of passion in a loved one's loins. If Passion Fruit Lobster Appetizer seems a bit too intense (perhaps you are cooking for a first date), you can substitute a different shellfish such as scallops.

Passion Fruit Lobster Appetizer

(Nicole Alper & Lynette Rohrer)

4 1-pound lobsters, already cooked with shells discarded

2 shallots

¾ cup rice wine vinegar

2 cups passion fruit juice

1 cup passion fruit liqueur, such as Alizé

8 ounces butter, cut into small cubes

4 cups tightly packed mixed greens

Caviar (enough for 8 small scoops to garnish lobster)

Salt and pepper to taste

In a nonreactive saucepan over moderately high heat, reduce the shallots and rice wine vinegar to half their original amount. Add the fruit juice and liqueur and reduce by half again. Reduce the heat under the sauce a bit and whisk in the butter, a little at a time, until it is all incorporated. Prepare eight appetizer plates, each with a small mound of mixed greens.

Warm the lobster in the sauce. Place ½ a lobster per person on each plate of greens and pour a bit of sauce over the top. Place a very small scoop of caviar on a central piece of lobster. Serves 8.

Sizzling Shrimp

2 tablespoons olive oil

1 tablespoon minced garlic clove

1 tablespoon chopped fresh rosemary

½ teaspoon cayenne pepper, or to taste

1 pound large shrimp, peeled and deveined

2 limes, halved

Combine the oil, garlic, rosemary, and cayenne in a large bowl. Add shrimp and toss to coat. Marinate at room temperature for 1 hour.

In a nonstick saucepan over medium-high heat, place the shrimp in one layer and cover with the rest of the marinade. Cook, turning once, for 4 to 8 minutes, depending on the size of the shrimp. Serve with lime wedges. Serves 4.

Black Truffle Soufflé
(Lynette Rohrer & Nicole Alper)

2 tablespoons butter

1 cup milk

3 tablespoons flour

1 black truffle

⅔ cup Swiss or Jarlsberg cheese, grated

3 eggs, separated

Pinch of mace

Salt and pepper to taste

¼ cup heavy cream

Preheat the oven to 350 degrees. Make a roux by melting the butter in a saucepan, adding the flour, and stirring to make a paste. Then add the milk a bit at a time, stirring constantly. Continue cooking and whisking for about 3½ minutes, until it thickens. Dice the truffle and add it and the cheese to the roux. Whisk in the egg yolks and season with mace, salt, and pepper. Whip the egg whites to stiff peaks and fold into the roux mixture. Fill six 4-ounce well buttered ramekins ¾ full.

The Power of Suggestion

Faith apparently plays a great part in the effectiveness of an aphrodisiac. When Madame Du Barry fed amber-spiked bonbons to the aging Louis XV, she was sure to mention, quite casually, that the recipe for those delicious tidbits was handed down by an Arabian sheik who not only satisfied a harem of 150 concubines, but also managed to deflower 80 virgins in a fortnight.

Place the ramekins in a pan and then fill the pan with boiling water so that it reaches halfway up the sides of the ramekins. Bake in the middle rack of the oven for 25 minutes. Remove them from the water bath; let cool. Run a knife around the edges of the ramekins. One at a time, cover with a small plate, invert the ramekin onto the plate, and rap sharply on the bottom to loosen the contents onto the plate. Then transfer each of the soufflés face up, to a baking dish large enough to hold them all so that they almost touch. Pour the cream around them and bake until lightly browned, about 10 to 12 minutes. Serves 6.

"Before I was born, my mother was in great agony of spirits and in a tragic situation. She could take no food except iced oysters and champagne. If people ask me when I began to dance, I reply, 'In my Mother's womb, probably as a result of the oysters and champagne—the food of Aphrodite.'"
—Isadora Duncan

Et Tu, Fungi, or Beware the Angry Cook

Those who control the cooking always have the opportunity to slip a little something extra into the stew. Perhaps that's why the famous poisoners of yore, particularly the Romans, were women. And perhaps the most famous poisoner of all was **Locusta**, who lived in Rome about 2,000 years ago, in the time of the Emperor Claudius.

Claudius, if you remember your classics (or your *Masterpiece Theatre*) was married to the wiley Agrippina the Younger in a purely political alliance. Agrippina detested the emperor, but managed to bide her time until her son Nero was old enough to rule. When the future fiddler turned seventeen, the empress decided to tarry no longer and called on Locusta to off Claudius. At this point in the story, history offers two versions. One story has it that Locusta served Claudius a dish of the fly agaric, a mushroom similar in appearance to the most prized mushroom of antiquity—the royal agaric—but with one crucial difference: it was highly poisonous. The dish did the trick and the fungus ever after was known as Caesar's mushroom.

Other historians say the above story is unlikely, that rather than poisonous mushrooms, Locusta served mushrooms (Claudius' favorite dish) laced with poison, which resulted in a variety of intestinal difficulties (he was also very drunk at the time), but not death. Fearing such a turn of events, Locusta then dipped a feather in poison and stuffed it down his throat. The second dose worked like a charm and Nero became emperor.

Rambunctious as we may be, we are not murderers, and so you will find only perfectly safe mushroom recipes here which you can enjoy without fear.

Sumptuous Stuffed Mushrooms

Mushrooms Duxelles

3 ounces chicken livers

4 cups mushrooms (wild, if available), diced

2 tablespoons butter

2 tablespoons minced shallots

Salt and pepper to taste

2 tablespoons cognac

———————

3 tablespoons cream

3 tablespoons fresh white bread crumbs

⅓ cup diced pancetta, sautéed until crisp

Salt and pepper to taste

1 teaspoon tarragon

6 mushrooms, about 3½″ wide cavity

3 tablespoons melted butter

2 tablespoons bleu cheese

Prepare the Duxelles: Squeeze out liquid from mushrooms by placing them in a clean towel and wringing it. Heat butter and sauté chicken livers and shallots on moderate heat. Add the mushrooms and cook for 3 to 4 minutes, stirring occasionally. Add the cognac and cook until it almost completely evaporates.

Blend the Duxelles with the cream. Add the bread crumbs and pancetta and mix. Season with salt, pepper, and tarragon.

Preheat the oven to 400 degrees. Brush whole mushroom caps with butter and spoon stuffing into them. Crumble a bit of bleu cheese on top of each mushroom and arrange in a baking dish. Bake for 20 minutes or until caps are tender. Serves 6.

"Always take a good look at what you're about to eat. It's not
so important to know what it is, but it's critical
to know what it was."
—Texas Bix Bender

Sultry Soups, Salads, and Side Dishes

Beer, the Housewife's Best Friend

Prior to the introduction of the potato, beer was second only to bread as the main source of nourishment for most central and northern Europeans. The average English family in the latter half of the seventeenth century, including children, drank three liters of beer per person per day. Breakfast usually consisted of beer soup, which was made from hot beer, butter, and a couple of eggs whisked together and poured over a roll or hunk of bread. It was apparently popular even among royalty. The Duchess Elisabeth Charlotte of Orleans, for example, wrote in a letter, "Tea makes me think of hay and dung, coffee of soot and lupine-seed, and chocolate is too sweet for me—it gives me a stomachache—I can't stand any of them. How much I would prefer a good beer soup, that wouldn't give me a stomachache."

As in ancient times, housewives were the brewers. They made the beverage at home for their own use; some also sold it to taverns; a lucky few even owned barrooms. One such woman was **Dionis Coffin**, a colonial tavern keeper in Newbury, Massachusetts, who was called before the local court in 1653 on a charge of selling her beer above the legal price. Feisty enough (or possibly inebriated enough) to fight City Hall, Coffin summoned several witnesses who swore that she used finer ingredients than the law required, thus proving her beer was worth a premium. The court relented and allowed the higher charge.

Here's her court-convincing recipe: "To Make Spruce Beer out of Shed Spruce. To one quart of shed spruce, [add] two gallons of cold water, and so in proportion to the quantity you wish to make. Then add one pint of molasses to every two gallons, let it boil 4 or 5 hours, and stand till it is lukewarm. Then put

one pint of yeast to ten gallons, let it work, then put into your cask and bring it up tight, and in two days it will be fit for use."

You might not want to imbibe Dionis' beer or eat old-fashioned beer soup, but in the name of beer-loving women everywhere, we've concocted the following soup that even Dionis would have approved of.

Bubbly Beer Cheese Soup

1 quart chicken broth

2½ pounds potatoes, coarsely chopped

1 small onion, diced

1 quart lowfat milk

4 tablespoons soy sauce

1 teaspoon pepper

¾ pound Cheddar cheese
(may be lower fat version), grated

1 cup beer

Paprika

"There is nothing like soup. It is by nature eccentric: no two are ever alike, unless of course you get your soup from cans."

—Laurie Colwin

In a large soup pot, bring the broth to a boil and add the potatoes and onion and simmer for 30 minutes. Remove the pot from the heat, allow to cool a bit, and add the milk.

In small batches, purée the mixture in a food processor and return to the pot. Add the soy sauce and pepper and stir well. On low heat, slowly bring soup back to simmer; then stir in the cheese. When the cheese is melted, add the beer, stir, ladle into bowls, and sprinkle paprika on top. Serves 6.

Don't Clam Up

The next time you have clam chowder, thank Ruth Alden Bass of Duxbury, Massachusetts. Ruth was just a starving colonist in the seventeenth century when she spied a pig rooting in the sand along the seashore. She followed suit and came up with a handful of clams. The enterprising Ruth decided that if they were good enough for Porky, they were good enough for her.

Angel with a Lariat

Canadian singer/songwriter **k.d. lang** has never allowed herself to be boxed in by others' definitions of who she is or should be (although, discussing her fans in an interview on *Bravo* she noted, "Like they say, I'm the Tom Jones of lesbians.") Perhaps the only lesbian country music singer in history (or at least the only one out of the closet), lang, with her powerful and sultry voice, has won many awards, including Grammys for Best Female Vocalist and for Best Vocal Collaboration for *Crying,* a duet with Roy Orbison. But just when music critics thought they had her pegged in the country music genre—a notorious bastion of sexism—lang switched gears and released *Ingenue.* The album's iconoclastic collection of love ballads, with nary a twang in sight, skyrocketed her to fame. Infamous, perhaps, was her *Vanity Fair*

cover, which depicted the daring chanteuse as a man, being given a shave by ultra-femme Cindy Crawford. Tongues wagged and voices tittered but lang just kept on singing (and chuckling, we suspect).

In keeping with her saucy persona, lang loves spicy food, as witnessed by the following recipe she contributed to *The Rock & Roll Cookbook*—a little number she calls her "constant craving." As you can see, it is a vegetarian dish, because lang eschews all meat—a choice that she says has raised more eyebrows than her sexual orientation.

Indonesian Salad with Spicy Peanut Dressing

3 tablespoons vegetable oil

Salt to taste

1 pound firm tofu, patted dry and cut
into ¼-inch cubes

2 small potatoes, boiled and cut
into bite-sized wedges

½ pound spinach, cleaned, steamed,
and chopped

½ small head green cabbage, shredded
and lightly steamed

½ pound mung bean sprouts, washed thoroughly

Dressing

4 cloves garlic

¼ cup roasted peanuts

5 teaspoons soy sauce or tamari

3 tablespoons lime or lemon juice

4 teaspoons brown sugar

¼ teaspoon cayenne pepper

2 tablespoons water

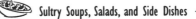

Heat the oil and salt in a medium frying pan over medium heat. Add the tofu in small batches and sauté until lightly browned on both sides, about 5 minutes. Remove with slotted spoon and drain on paper towel.

Combine the tofu, potatoes, spinach, and cabbage together and arrange on 6 plates. Prepare the dressing by placing all the ingredients in a blender and blending until smooth. If the dressing seems too thick, add another teaspoon of water. Top the salad with the sprouts and dressing and serve immediately. Serves 6.

Just Say No

The first food boycott in history was organized by abolitionists against sugar because its harvesting was done by slaves. By forgoing sugar or by purchasing sugar from the East Indies (which did not use slaves), the Anti-Saccharite Society claimed that eight families that each typically used five pounds of sugar a week would, over the course of twenty years, prevent the slavery or murder of one hundred people. One supporter of the boycott was Mrs. B. Henderson, a businesswoman in London who sold sugar basins with gold letters that proclaimed "East India sugar not made by slaves."

The Olive Matriarch

he California ripe olive industry, which along with growers in Spain, brings canned black pitted olives to the world (did everyone have these morsels only at Thanksgiving and Christmas as a child or was it just us?) was launched by wild woman **Freda Ehmann**. Not much is known about Ehmann except that she was fond of olives and had ambitions that were larger than those of the ordinary farmer. At the early part of the twentieth century, Freda turned a modest twenty-acre spread into the first modern olive-processing plant. In recent years, such olives have gone out of favor among foodies, displaced by the more exotic Kalamata, Niçoise, Picholine, and Gaeta, to name just a few. Even we branch out a bit here and present a couple of recipes with these newcomers. But they are all offered in honor of Freda Ehmann, fondly known as the Mother of the California Ripe Olive.

Olive Soup

2 tablespoons olive oil

1 cup chopped onion

3 cloves garlic, chopped

1 stalk celery, diced

2 teaspoons dried basil

1 small zucchini, diced

Salt and pepper to taste

3 cups chicken broth or water

1 14½-ounce can chopped tomatoes

¼ cup dry red wine

2 cups cooked white beans

1 cup chopped ripe black olives

1 tablespoon lemon juice

Heat the oil in a large soup pot over medium heat. Add onion, garlic, celery, and basil and cook until vegetables start to soften, about 10 minutes. Add zucchini and sauté 5 more minutes. Add remaining ingredients, stir, and simmer over low heat for 15 minutes. Serves 6.

Warm Broccoli Salad

1 large bunch broccoli

1 to 2 tablespoons virgin olive oil

1 garlic clove, crushed

10 Kalamata olives, coarsely chopped

3 tablespoons diced roasted peppers

1 tablespoon finely chopped fresh parsley

2 ounces feta cheese

Freshly ground black pepper

Cut the stalks off the broccoli and cut the tops into medium-size florets. Steam the broccoli until it is cooked but still crunchy, about ten minutes or so.

Heat the oil in a large pan and add the garlic. When the garlic has browned, add the broccoli, olives, peppers, and parsley. Sauté over medium-high heat until warmed through. Place on a serving dish, crumble cheese over the top, and add pepper to taste. Serve immediately. Serves 4.

Moroccan Orange and Olive Salad

2 cloves garlic, minced

¼ teaspoon salt, or to taste

1 teaspoon sweet paprika

½ cup minced fresh parsley

½ teaspoon ground cumin

Dash of cayenne pepper

2 tablespoons olive oil

5 navel oranges, peeled and sliced

¾ cup black oil-cured olives

Lettuce leaves

Whisk the first 7 ingredients together in a small bowl.

Line a serving platter with lettuce leaves and arrange orange slices attractively. Scatter the olives and drizzle dressing over all. Refrigerate; serve cold. Serves 4 to 6.

Penne Pesto Pasta Salad

(Nicole Alper & Lynette Rohrer)

Salad

6 ounces dried penne pasta, cooked 12 minutes and drained

1 4-ounce jar of pimentos, drained and sliced into strips

½ cup sliced ripe olives

½ cup diced green chilies

1 6½-ounce jar marinated artichoke hearts,
drained and chopped

4 ounces feta cheese, crumbled

Pesto Dressing

1 cup basil leaves (reserve one flower)

3 cloves garlic

½ cup pinenuts

½ cup extra-virgin olive oil

½ cup Parmesan cheese (reserve 2 tablespoons)

1 teaspoon salt

1 teaspoon white pepper

Prepare the pasta according to the package directions; drain.

Combine all the salad ingredients in a large bowl.

Combine the basil, garlic, and nuts in food processor. While the machine is still running, add the oil in a very thin stream. When all the oil is incorporated, turn off the food processor and stir in the ½ cup cheese, salt, and pepper. Add the pesto to the salad mixture and combine thoroughly. Transfer the pasta salad to a serving bowl, top with the remaining 2 tablespoons cheese, and garnish with a basil flower. Serve at room temperature or chilled. Serves 6.

The Real Secret of Southern Cooking

Among the most unsung heroes in the kitchen are the slaves who produced superb dishes under the most trying of circumstances. For example, ex-slave Gustavus Vassa noted in his journal that he once saw a Virginia slave cook busily at work in the kitchen with a heavy iron muzzle around her head. The purpose of this contraption was to prohibit slaves from eating the master's food during preparation. And because slaveholders so often mistreated their slaves, they lived in fear of being poisoned. As a result, whites concocted laws prescribing death by torturous methods to prevent a dissatisfied cook from disposing of her owner and his family.

Despite such hardships, slave cooks managed to create an entire cuisine. In most areas, teaching slaves to read or write was a severe offense, so there are no accurate written records of their dishes. Recipes were either memorized and passed down through the generations of cooks, or were read to the slaves by the mistress of the house, if she herself could read. Mrs. Thomas Jefferson was one of the few fortunate female members of society who was educated, and a former slave of the presidential family recalled that Mrs. Jefferson would read long recipes to her cooks that they would then follow.

Today, organizations such as the National Council of Negro Women in *Celebrating Our Mothers' Kitchens* and individuals such as Jessica B. Harris, author of many cookbooks including *From Quingombo to Gumbo: African American Heritage Cooking,* have sought to preserve authentic African-American recipes. In that same vein, we offer Hoppin' John, believed to have originated in Africa, and traditionally served on New Year's Day throughout Black America. It is a wonderful comfort food, perfect as a side dish.

Hoppin' John

2 tablespoons olive oil

1 large onion, chopped

1 smoked ham hock

2½ quarts water

1 16-ounce package dried black-eyed peas, rinsed

2 teaspoons dried thyme

2 tablespoons chopped fresh parsley

2 cups white rice

Heat the oil in a large soup pot over medium-high heat. Add the onion and ham hock and cook, stirring, until the onion is wilted. Add 2 quarts of cold water, the peas, thyme, and parsley. Bring to a boil, then cover and simmer for 2½ hours or until tender.

Remove the ham hocks from the stock and let sit until cool enough to handle. Remove the meat from the bone and shred. Discard the bone; return the ham to the pot. Add the rice and the remaining 2 cups of water. Return to a boil; then lower heat and simmer, covered, for 20 minutes or until rice is cooked. Serves 8.

"If a vegetable is meant to be eaten raw, then it should be raw,
but if not, it should be honestly cooked."
—Edna Lewis, cook

We've Got You, Babe

Cher—"I'm a gutsy kind of gal"—might be best known for her outrageous outfits, tough-looking lovers, bedroom eyes, and tattoos. But as her fellow wild women know, she isn't all skin-tight Bob Mackie dresses and feathers; she does have a get-down-to-business side. Her entertainment accomplishments include Top 40 music singles, a hit TV series with then-husband Sonny Bono, and several critically-acclaimed films including *Silkwood*, *Come Back to the Five and Dime, Jimmy Dean, Jimmy Dean,* and *Moonstruck,* for which she won the Best Actress Academy Award. In the kitchen, Cher loves to make Salade Niçoise, a version of which we offer here. In keeping with Cher's health consciousness, the dressing is made with cold chicken broth, which cuts down considerably on the need for oil, and the traditional eggs are omitted.

Salade Niçoise

Olive oil to brush on fish

Freshly ground black pepper

Pinch of dried tarragon

4 5- to 6-ounce ahi tuna steaks

Dressing

⅓ cup balsamic vinegar

½ teaspoon Dijon-style mustard

¼ cup cold chicken broth, fat skimmed off

2 tablespoons capers

3 tablespoons chopped anchovies

½ cup extra-virgin olive oil

Salt and pepper

---

8 tiny red new potatoes, halved and cooked

½ red onion, minced

1 head romaine lettuce, cut and washed

2 tomatoes, sliced

1 cup green beans, trimmed and blanched

¼ cup Niçoise olives

Preheat the broiler or barbecue. Combine the olive oil, pepper, and tarragon and brush on the tuna. Grill to desired doneness in broiler or on barbecue, about 5 to 10 minutes, depending on thickness. Cut into 4 slices.

Make the dressing: Mix all ingredients together, except olive oil. Slowly whisk in olive oil until fully incorporated. Adjust seasoning with salt and pepper to taste. In a large bowl, toss potatoes with ⅓ of the dressing and the onion.

Arrange the potatoes around the edge of a large serving plate. Mound the lettuce in the center, and arrange the tomatoes, green beans, and olives. Place the tuna on top. Drizzle the remaining dressing over the top. Serves 4.

Mother's Imaginary Friend

One of the most widely known female cooks is not actually a woman, but a man-made marketing device. **"Betty Crocker"** is not a woman, but a name owned by General Mills and used by home economists in the Betty Crocker Home Service Department, which was established in 1921. The company describes Ms. Crocker's "birth":

"The Betty Crocker Kitchens were created in order to give help to the hundreds of American housewives who wrote to General Mills with questions concerning their cooking problems. The name Betty Crocker was chosen because it was felt that these letters should be answered in a personal manner and should be answered by a woman. The surname 'Crocker' was chosen because it had belonged to the enormously popular secretary and director of the Washburn Crosby Company, William G. Crocker. The name 'Betty' was chosen because it seemed to be one of the most familiar and most companionable of all family nicknames. The original Betty Crocker portrait was painted by the artist Neysa M. McMein."

As you can see, Betty has changed over the years, but unlike real women, she keeps getting younger. Her most recent "facelift," in response to the ethnic diversity of the United States, was designed to give her a less "Waspy" look. What do you think?

"People who loathe the idea of a salad are very like those who claim not to like perfume: they just haven't met the right one."
—Miriam Polunin

1955

1968

1965

1986

Plastic surgery: The eighth version of Betty Crocker was introduced on her 75th birthday. 75 women's features were blended to create the new Betty.

Elegant Tossed Salad

Cheese-Mustard Dressing

2 tablespoons olive or vegetable oil

1 tablespoon red wine vinegar

2 teaspoons grated Parmesan cheese

2 teaspoons Dijon-style mustard

¼ teaspoon salt

---

4 slices French bread, each ½ inch thick

2 large cloves garlic, cut lengthwise into halves

2 tablespoons olive or vegetable oil

4 cups watercress

1½ cups fresh mushrooms, washed and sliced

1 medium leek, thinly sliced

½ head Boston lettuce, torn into bite-size pieces

½ small bunch romaine, torn into bite-size pieces

Prepare Cheese-Mustard Dressing by shaking all ingredients in tightly covered container, and refrigerating at least 1 hour.

Tear bread into ½-inch pieces. Cook garlic in oil in 8-inch skillet over medium heat, stirring frequently until garlic is deep golden brown; remove garlic and discard. Add bread to oil. Cook and stir until bread is golden brown and crusty; cool.

Shake Cheese-Mustard Dressing; toss with watercress, mushrooms, leeks, lettuces and romaine. Sprinkle with bread. Makes 8 servings.

The Dangers of Cross-Dressing

oan of Arc was certainly a woman who marched to the beat of her own drum—or in this case, her own voices. A shepherdess from Lorraine, France, in the early 1400s, at age seventeen she began to hear voices and see visions of Archangel Michael, Saint Catherine, and Saint Margaret, who told her that since France was lost to the British by a woman (Isabelle of Bavaria) it must be saved by a virgin, specifically Joan, and that the dauphin (the French heir to the throne) must be reinstalled. After resisting the voices for three years and then suffering the ridicule of the French aristocracy, she finally convinced the dauphin in 1429 to provide her with a small army. She wrote a letter to the British, boasting, "I am a chieftain of war and whenever I meet your followers in France I will drive them out; if they will not obey, I will put them all to death."

Dressed as a soldier and equipped with a sword, she led an army of 4,000 men that swiftly drove the English out of France and placed the dauphin, now Charles VII, on the throne. Upon which poet Christine de Pisan wrote verses comparing Joan to such biblical figures as Esther, Judith, and Deborah. One of these verses reads, in part: "the kingdom, once lost,/Was recovered by a woman,/A thing that men could not do." Two years later—too uppity for the churchmen of the time—she was burned at the stake as a heretic, the charges including "inappropriate

physical appearance." Not even Charles lifted a finger to save her. What goes around, comes around, though—in 1920, the Vatican declared her a saint.

As she prepared for battle, Joan had wine and water mixed in a silver cup, into which she put five or six *soupes,* or slices of bread, which had been dipped into meat and vegetable juices. She ate nothing else.

While more ascetic than the majority of eaters at the time, Joan was following an honorable French tradition with her soggy bread. Up until the fifteenth century, there were no such things as dishes. Every diner had a trencher (from the Old French *tranchier,* to cut), which was a thick slice of stale bread measuring about six inches by four that served as an absorbent plate. By Joan's time, however, the bread trencher was being superseded by a square of wood with a circular depression in the middle—which ultimately evolved into a soup bowl, with soupes inside.

Soup in the modern sense was introduced to France around 1650, with the soup itself becoming more important than the soupes it contained. Nonetheless, no cookbook that seeks to pay homage to this wild woman would be complete without a couple of hearty peasant bread soups, the most famous of which, of course, is French Onion Soup. The version presented here was made for centuries at Les Halles, a huge Parisian market where traditionally, just after midnight, farmers would truck their wares in from the countryside to the market. By 2:00 A.M., restaurant owners and shopkeepers would arrive to buy ingredients for the day. A ring of restaurants sprang up around the markets and, because they were open all night, they became the after-hours stopover for theatergoers and other night owls. And because onion soup was believed to be an antidote to a hangover, all the restaurants in the area began serving it. Revelers typically ended an evening with a steaming bowl at Les Halles.

Onion Soup Les Halles

1 pound white onions, thinly sliced

2 cups dry white wine

2 tablespoons butter

*6 cups unsalted beef broth or 5 cups salted broth
diluted with 1 cup of water*

6 slices stale French bread, cut ½ inch thick

2 cups freshly grated Gruyère cheese (about ½ pound)

Preheat the oven to 425 degrees. In a medium flameproof dish, combine the onions, wine, and butter. Bake uncovered, stirring once or twice, until the onions are very soft and most of the liquid is evaporated, about 1 hour. Remove from the oven and set aside.

In a large saucepan, bring the broth to a boil. Preheat the broiler with the rack about 6 inches from the heat. Arrange six ovenproof soup bowls on a baking sheet. Evenly distribute the onions among the bowls and cover completely with broth. Place a round of bread on top of each. Sprinkle the cheese over the breads. Place the baking sheet under the broiler and broil until the cheese is lightly browned, about 2 minutes. Serves 6.

"When the talk turns to eating, a subject of the greatest importance,
only fools and sick men don't give it the attention it deserves."
—Laura Esquivel

Tomato Bread Soup

2 tablespoons olive oil

2 cloves garlic, pressed

½ cup diced onion

¼ cup coarsely chopped fresh basil

3 pounds ripe tomatoes, chopped, with juices

2 cups chicken broth or water

Salt and pepper to taste

½ sourdough baguette, cut into ½-inch slices

2 tablespoons grated Parmesan cheese

Heat the oil in a soup pot and sauté the garlic and onion over medium-low heat, about 10 minutes. Add the basil, tomatoes, and broth; season with salt and pepper, and simmer over medium-low heat for about 10 minutes.

Dirty Looks Will Not Be Tolerated at the Royal Table

Marguerite de Valois, the first wife of Henri IV of France, introduced long-handled spoons at court to minimize spillage on the very high collars that were in fashion at the time.

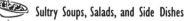

Break up the bread and stir it into the soup. Remove from the heat and let rest, covered, for one hour. Add more liquid if it seems too thick, and reheat just before serving until warm. Stir in the cheese, and serve at once. Serves 4.

You Just Can't Say No to the Gal with the Toaster Under Her Arm

In 1925, the first automatic toaster for home use came on the market. Though it was selling for a pricey twelve dollars and fifty cents (as compared to the two-dollar flip-flop models previously available, which heated just one side of the bread at a time), Toastmaster's sales force—ladies who went door to door, carrying a loaf of bread under one arm, and a Toastmaster under the other for handy demonstrations—swiftly persuaded Americans that they couldn't live without it.

The Star Who Created an Unusual Stir

French actress **Sarah Bernhardt** (1844–1923), or "the Divine Sarah," as her fervent followers called her, was in actuality a difficult, demanding, and impatient person, who, when touring the United States, often complained loudly that she found American food "unspeakably awful." According to Douglas Meldrum in *The Night 2000 Men Came to Dinner,* "she had some strange ideas about cooking and insisted on stirring bouillabaisse with a red-hot poker for reasons she alone understood."

You don't need a poker to make this French delight (though you could try Bernhardt's use of the seafood shells as spoons). Our version follows the traditional recipe, which calls for the soup and the fish to be served separately. It's best to use at least four different kinds of fish.

Bouillabaisse

1 small lobster or crab

4 pounds fish fillets, half firm- and half tender-fleshed, kept separate

1 large onion, chopped

1 large tomato, peeled, seeded, and chopped

3 cloves garlic, chopped

1 bay leaf

1 to 2 sprigs parsley

1 small piece of fennel bulb, sliced

1 small piece orange peel, about 2 inches long

½ cup olive oil

1 teaspoon salt

½ teaspoon pepper

Several threads saffron

2 cooked and peeled potatoes, kept warm

18 pieces stale French bread

2 tablespoons chopped fresh parsley

In a deep stock pot with a tight-fitting lid, place the lobster or crab and enough water to cover. When the shellfish turns red, reserve the cooking liquid and discard all shells except for the claws.

In a heatproof casserole with cover, place onion, tomato, garlic, bay leaf, parsley, fennel, orange peel, poached shellfish, and the firm-fleshed fish. Moisten with olive oil and add salt, pepper, and saffron. Cover and marinate in the refrigerator for several hours.

Add to casserole the reserved shellfish liquid and enough water to cover the fish. Bring to a boil. Cook for approximately 7 minutes. Then add the tender-fleshed fish and continue boiling for another 7 to 10 minutes or until all the fish is cooked but not falling apart

Put 1 slice of bread into each diner's soup bowl; put the remainder in a basket on the table. With a slotted spoon, carefully remove the fish from the pot and arrange it attractively on a platter with the potatoes. Place the platter on the table. Strain the broth into a deep soup tureen, add the claws of the lobster or crab, and sprinkle with parsley. Transfer the tureen to the table and ladle from it a bit of broth over the bread in each soup bowl. Serves 6.

"One cannot think well, love well, sleep well, if one has not dined well."

—Virginia Woolf

Another Take on French Fish Soup

In her high school years, Zelda Sayre won more hearts than any other young lady. Her popularity with the wartime soldiers allowed her to collect one cigar box full of their insignias. When Zelda met F. Scott Fitzgerald, however, all of this ended. Zelda and Scott began to live a wild life full of parties and pranks. After several years of this carefree lifestyle, Zelda began to feel the need to do something all her own. She first tried ballet, and when this failed to fulfill her, she switched to writing. Unfortunately, her husband did not support her having any sort of career and she ultimately ended up in a mental institution. In her one novel, *Save Me the Waltz*, Zelda describes a type of fish soup that supposedly contains pearls, though in truth the pearls are lobster eyes.

The Sparring Chefs

n 1977, **Sheila Lukins** and **Julee Russo** opened the Silver Palate, a take-out store in New York City which became one of the country's first high-profile, wildly successful female-owned businesses. Lukins did the cooking; Russo handled the marketing. Responsible for popularizing pesto, sun-dried tomatoes, and raspberry vinaigrette—at least on the East Coast—they were known not only for their fabulous food, but for their famous customers, including John Lennon and Yoko Ono, who bought a pecan pie every day until his death.

Lukins and Russo seemed an invincible team. They did three bestselling cookbooks together in the 1980s, and began a recipe column in *Parade Magazine* (which Lukins now does solo). But in 1985 they lost ownership of the Silver Palate to a larger company, having failed to get a loan to expand the business. Parting ways, they accepted separate book deals amid rumors that it was only Lukins who knew how to cook, and Russo started a newsletter, *Cook's Notes*. In 1991, Lukins suffered a massive stroke. Two weeks later, Russo sent a letter to her newsletter subscribers, blaming a late issue on Lukins' illness. Lukins was furious; they hadn't been in touch in ages and she didn't want what she felt to be Russo's ineptitude placed on her. Russo blamed the letter on her secretary; however, the secretary called Lukins to assure her that Russo had indeed dictated the letter to her.

All of this was dutifully reported in the press when in 1994 both solo cookbooks appeared: Russo's, the lowfat *Great Good Food*, was savaged by food critics who complained that the quantities in many recipes were so off that there was no way she could have tested them. Russo responded to press accusations that she couldn't cook in an oblique fashion, saying in *Vanity Fair*, "I'm not interested in fighting in public . . . We just have different interests at this point. I haven't cooked with salt in fifteen years."

On the other hand, Lukins' book, the *All Around the World Cookbook,* which she managed to do by traveling around the globe despite lingering impairments from her stroke, garnered lavish praise for her unique interpretation of many classics. Needless to say, they do not exchange holiday cards. We decided to present a recipe from each of these feuding females. We tested them and found both to be tasty. But as to which is better—you be the judge.

Garlic-Fried Greens
(from Julee Russo's *Great Good Food*)

½ cup golden raisins

2 tablespoons sherry

1 teaspoon olive oil

10 garlic cloves, slivered

3 pounds tender young greens (such as arugula, spinach, dandelion, or young turnip tops, or a combination), washed and trimmed

Freshly ground pepper

¼ cup toasted pine nuts or slivered almonds

In a small skillet, heat the raisins in the sherry, plump for 30 minutes.

In a very large skillet, heat the oil over medium heat. Add the garlic and sauté for 1 minute. Turn the heat to medium-high. Add the greens and cover; cook for 30 to 40 seconds. Remove the lid, toss the greens with a

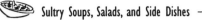

fork, replace the lid, and cook for 1 minute, tossing several times. Some greens may take longer to cook.

Pour the raisins and sherry over the greens. Season generously with pepper. Add the pine nuts and toss. Serve immediately. Serves 6.

Madras Chicken Salad
(from Sheila Lukins' *All Around the World Cookbook*)

Dressing

1 cup mayonnaise

1 cup nonfat plain yogurt

2 tablespoons curry powder

⅛ teaspoon ground turmeric

½ cup toasted shredded coconut

¼ cup mango chutney, finely chopped

Poached Chicken

1 carrot, halved

1 rib celery with leaves, halved

4 sprigs flat-leaf parsley

4 black peppercorns

1 bay leaf

8 cups water

4 whole boneless, skinless chicken breasts
(about 3 pounds total)

Salad

1 cup halved red seedless grapes

2 ribs celery, cut into ¼-inch dice

1 Granny Smith apple, cored and cut into ¼-inch dice

½ cup roasted peanuts

2 tablespoons chopped fresh mint leaves, for garnish

For the dressing, stir all the ingredients together and set aside.

For the poached chicken, place the carrot, celery, parsley, peppercorns, bay leaf, and water in a large pot and bring to a boil. Add the chicken breasts and simmer uncovered until cooked through, about 10 minutes. Remove from the cooking liquid, and let stand until cool enough to handle. Cut into 1-inch cubes, removing any cartilage.

For the salad, combine the chicken cubes, grapes, celery, apple, and peanuts in a large bowl. Add the curry dressing and combine well.

Refrigerate for at least 2 hours before serving to allow the flavors to meld. Sprinkle with chopped mint just before serving. Serves 8.

Invading the Male Bastion of the Commercial Kitchen

"Anyone who's ever claimed that a woman's place is in the kitchen has never visited a restaurant," writes Graham Rayman in the December 1995 issue of *Working Woman*. "Most chefs are men, and a lack of basic employee benefits, like health insurance, pension and retirement plans and maternity leave, helps keep it that way."

In 1993, Anne Rosenzweig, founder and chef of the acclaimed Arcadia in New York, joined Barbara Tropp of San Francisco's China Moon Cafe and eight other women to found the International Association of Women Chefs and Restaurateurs (IAWCR). The group, headquartered in San Francisco, helps provide networking and employment possibilities for women interested in advancing their career in the cooking industry. The organization has 1,200 members and is in the process of developing several programs, including a mentor program and an automated job bank. Currently, the IAWCR publishes a quarterly newsletter that lists job opportunities. (For information, call 415-362-7336.)

IAWCR cofounder **Barbara Tropp** is a Chinese scholar, a well-known cooking teacher, and the author of *The Modern Art of Chinese Cooking,* the definitive book on Chinese cooking techniques. Acclaimed by the *San Francisco Chronicle* as "the Julia Child of the Chinese kitchen," she is best known as the owner of the popular China Moon Cafe in San Francisco, where she marries Chinese tastes and techniques with California flair.

Here we offer several recipes inspired by Tropp's approach to cooking. In honor of the fact that women are invading commercial kitchens all over the world, we also feature a recipe by Vancouver chef **Diane Clement,** who concocted her Les Dames Pacific Northwest Salad for a fundraiser in honor of Les Dames d'Escoffier, a Canadian networking group of women in the food industry.

Ginger Hot and Sour Soup

2 cups boiling water

1½ ounces dried shiitake mushrooms

1½ tablespoons sesame oil

3 tablespoons minced fresh ginger

6 cups chicken broth

1 small Chinese cabbage, shredded

1 ounce angel hair pasta, broken in half

2 tablespoons soy sauce

Pinch of sugar

½ to 1 teaspoon crushed red pepper

½ package extra-firm tofu, diced

¼ cup canned bamboo shoots

5 to 10 tablespoons rice vinegar

2 tablespoons cornstarch

Combine the boiling water and mushrooms in a bowl. Let steep for 15 minutes, until mushrooms soften. Remove mushrooms, reserving mushroom water; rinse mushrooms well, squeeze dry, and thinly slice the caps, discarding stems.

Heat oil in a large soup pot over high heat. Add the ginger and stir-fry for 30 seconds. Pour in the chicken broth and the reserved mushroom water, leaving behind any sediment. Bring to boil. Add the cabbage, pasta, soy sauce, and sugar. Add the red pepper, to taste, depending on how hot you want it. Reduce the heat to medium; cover, and simmer 5 minutes.

In a small bowl, combine 5 tablespoons rice vinegar with the cornstarch. Add the cornstarch mixture, tofu, bamboo shoots, and mushrooms to the pot. Stir well and simmer until heated through. Taste and adjust seasoning with more red pepper or vinegar, if desired. Serves 4.

Stir-Fried Red Cabbage

2½ tablespoons peanut oil

1 1-inch-wide slice fresh ginger, grated

1 pound red cabbage, cored and shredded

2 to 3 tablespoons chicken or vegetable stock, if needed

4 scallions, cut into 1-inch pieces

Heat a wok or a heavy skillet over high heat until very hot. Add oil to coat. When oil is very hot, add the ginger and stir until golden brown. Add the cabbage and stir-fry for about 7 minutes, until the cabbage is softened. If it seems too dry, add a little stock to moisten. When the cabbage is done, add the scallions and stir-fry for 1 minute. Serves 4.

Asian Couscous

1½ cups boiling water

1 ounce dried shiitake mushrooms

½ cup green beans, cut into 2-inch lengths

1 cup broccoli florets

¼ cup rice wine vinegar

¼ cup soy sauce

1 tablespoon peanut oil

2 tablespoons sesame oil

1½ tablespoons minced garlic

1 teaspoon sugar

1½ tablespoons minced fresh ginger

1 cup instant couscous

1 small red onion, chopped

1 cup snow peas

½ cup Chinese cabbage, shredded

½ green or red pepper, cut into thin strips

Combine the boiling water and mushrooms in a bowl. Let steep in hot water for 15 minutes, until mushrooms soften. Remove mushrooms; rinse mushrooms well, squeeze dry, and thinly slice the caps, discarding water and stems.

Meanwhile, blanch the beans and broccoli in boiling water for 2 minutes. Drain, rinse under cold water and drain well. Set aside.

Combine the next 7 ingredients in a small bowl until well blended. Make couscous according to the package directions and allow to sit, covered, while vegetables cook.

Heat a large skillet or wok over high heat and add ¼ cup of the soy sauce mixture. When bubbling, add beans, broccoli, and remaining vegetables, except mushrooms, and stir-fry until crisp-tender, about 5 minutes. Add the mushrooms and the remaining soy sauce; toss to coat. Heat just until mushrooms are heated through, about 1 minute. Mound couscous on a platter and scatter vegetables on top. Serves 6 as a side dish.

Les Dames Pacific Northwest Salad

½ pound smoked salmon (Diane Clement recommends Westcoast
Select Indian Candy, "the best in the world")

3 cups mixed wild mushrooms, such as
shiitake, oyster, chanterelle

2 tablespoons olive oil

2 tablespoons butter

Freshly ground pepper to taste

1 pound mixed greens

8 ounces chèvre, crumbled

Maple Balsamic Vinaigrette

5 tablespoons balsamic vinegar

1 teaspoon Dijon-style mustard

3 tablespoons maple syrup

Pepper to taste

1 cup olive oil or a mix of olive and canola oils

Peel the skin off the salmon, slice in finger-length strips, and set aside. Remove the stems from the mushrooms and slice the tops thinly.

Just before serving, heat the oil and butter in a skillet, add the mushrooms and sauté until softened. Add pepper to taste and keep warm. Make the Maple Balsamic Vinaigrette by whisking the ingredients together in order given.

Divide the greens evenly among six salad plates, mounding them high. Sprinkle about 2 tablespoons of chèvre over the greens. Stand the salmon strips upright against the greens, arranging them around the mound. Divide the mushrooms evenly around the outside of each plate. Drizzle a little of the warm vinaigrette over the greens and serve immediately. Pass more dressing, if desired. Serves 6.

"It is hard to work with those [in the food industry] who see women as nothing more than 'edible flowers' but when it is crunch time, the proof of our skills, knowledge, and experience is on the plate."

—Sosinna Degefu, member of the International Association of Women Chefs and Restaurateurs

Pass the Toque

Women have been shaking up commercial kitchens a great deal in the past two decades. Until recently there were very few full-fledged women chefs and "you could count entrepreneurs such as Mrs. Fields and Alice Waters on the fingers of one hand," writes Mimi Sheraton in the January 1996 issue of *New Woman*. Not any more! A few of the hot, food-oriented females who've best proven they can stand the heat include:

- Barbara Smith, restaurateur (she owns B. Smith's in New York City and Washington, DC), cookbook author, and television show host dubbed the "Martha Stewart of Soul" by the *New York Times*;

- Cindy Pawlcyn, chef and corporate partner in Real Restaurants, for which she created such San Francisco Bay Area favorites as the Fog City Diner (which also has branches in Dallas and Las Vegas), Roti, Bix, and Tra Vigne; and

- Sarah Stegner, chef at Chicago's exclusive Ritz Carlton's Four Seasons Regent Hotel, who won the James Beard Foundation's Rising Star Chef of the Year Award in 1994.

There's Not a Safe Tomato South of the Mason-Dixon Line

"When the movie *Fried Green Tomatoes* came out it suddenly seemed that every cafe, restaurant, and cafeteria started serving fried green tomatoes," writes author Fannie Flagg in *Fannie Flagg's Original Whistle Stop Cafe Cookbook.* (Flagg also penned the novel upon which the movie was based.) "One night we were in Atlanta and my friend, Dan Martin, took me to an exclusive, decidedly elegant restaurant. The captain, after announcing a long list of exotic entrees, announced that no dinner would be complete without their specialty, fried green tomatoes.

"Dan whispered to me: 'I wish you had a piece of the tomato market—I heard the prices have quadrupled and restaurant buyers are having fistfights trying to get the best green ones.' I can't help feeling a little bit guilty, however. I have caused thousands of poor little green tomatoes to go to an early picking. But I couldn't help it. They taste so good. People ask me why I think they are popular in the South. Like most of this food, it really started getting to be a popular dish during the Depression. People would fry up most anything and pretend it was meat or fish, and actually as it turned out, a pitcher full of sweet iced tea and a plate of fried green tomatoes turned out to be a delightfully tasty and light summer supper on nights when it was so hot you didn't feel like having a big heavy meal.

"So some hot summer night, fix yourself a plate of fried green tomatoes and a pitcher of iced tea, and go out on the screen porch and watch the fireflies and listen to the sounds of night birds and the crickets instead of the six o'clock news. You'll never regret it."

Fried Green Tomatoes

¾ cup self-rising flour

¼ cup cornmeal

¼ teaspoon salt

¼ teaspoon pepper

¾ cup milk

3 to 4 green tomatoes, cut into ¼-inch slices

Vegetable oil

Combine the first 5 ingredients; mix until smooth. Add additional milk to thin, if necessary; batter should resemble pancake batter. Working in batches, dip tomato slices into batter, allowing excess batter to drip back into bowl. Fry in 2 inches hot oil (375 degrees) in a large heavy skillet until browned, turning once carefully with tongs. Transfer to colander to drain. Serves 3 to 4.

Fannie Grows into Her Role

"In making the movie *Fried Green Tomatoes*," explains bona fide wild woman Fannie Flagg, "some of the best times were when Kathy Bates—who is from Memphis and knows good food—and I used to sneak off and eat some of that wonderful Georgia cooking. I had a small part in the film and was unfortunately fitted before the movie started. When it was time to film my scene, the dress had suddenly shrunk several sizes. I think it was the Georgia heat that caused it. That's my story and I'm sticking to it."

Women Even Invented
Freeze-Dried Potatoes!

O n the west coast of what is now Peru, there once were small oases where fifty streams came down from the Andes; this is where pre-Columbian peoples lived, using the natural irrigation system to create prosperous societies ruled by the highland Inca. The men harvested fish from the sea while the women cultivated lima beans, corn, and a few root crops such as potatoes. Since food preservation was a problem—there was no such thing as refrigeration, of course—these resourceful females took advantage of the freezing nights of the Andean mountains to create freeze-dried potatoes, which would keep indefinitely. Potatoes were grown in the valley, harvested, and then carried up to the highlands where they were spread out overnight to freeze. When they thawed out in the morning sun, the women would trample on them, squeezing out the water. After about three of these freezings and thawings, all the water had been extracted from the potatoes and voilà! Ready to store for the winter.

Fortunately, unless you are on a camping trip, food preservation is not such an issue anymore and we can enjoy potatoes that haven't had the life wrung out of them. Here are a few that are more interesting than the old-fashioned fried or baked stuffed variety.

Garlic Mashed Potatoes

6 russet potatoes, about 1¾ pounds, peeled

6 whole garlic cloves, peeled

1⅓ cups milk, warmed (lowfat or nonfat milk, if desired)

½ cup finely chopped fresh parsley

Salt and pepper to taste

Cut potatoes crosswise into ¼-inch pieces. Place in a large saucepan with the garlic and add enough water to cover. Bring to a boil over high heat, then reduce heat and simmer 15 minutes or until potatoes are tender. Drain; then return the potatoes to the pot. Mash together the potatoes and garlic. Add the milk, blend until creamy and fluffy; then add the parsley, salt, and pepper. Serve immediately. Serves 4.

Sweet Potato Gratin

(Lynette Rohrer)

3 sweet potatoes, peeled and sliced thin

1 tablespoon finely minced fresh sage

1 cup cream

½ cup grated Jarlsberg cheese

Preheat oven to 350 degrees. In a buttered casserole dish, overlap the potato slices in a single layer. Sprinkle with half of the sage and pour half of the cream over. Add another layer of potatoes and top with the rest of the sage and cream. Sprinkle with cheese. Bake for 40 minutes, or until the potatoes are cooked and the top is bubbly. Serves 6.

"A recipe is only a theme which an intelligent cook can play each time with a variation."

—Madame Benoit

Vegetable Gratin

**(by wild woman chef and former Olympian sprinter Diane Clement
of the Tomato Fresh Food Cafe in Vancouver, British Columbia)**

8 small red or white potatoes, thinly sliced

2 small zucchini, thinly sliced

7 roma tomatoes, thinly sliced

6 tablespoons grated Parmesan cheese

Dried basil and oregano, to taste

⅓ cup fresh basil, chopped

⅓ cup chicken stock

Olive oil

Love That Cool Air

Incan women were not the only females thinking about food preservation. Eygptian housewives had similar concerns and, around 3000 B.C., managed to figure out how to make ice in a baking hot country! According to Charles Panati in *Extraordinary Origins of Everyday Things*, "[a]round sundown, Eygptian women placed water in shallow clay trays on a bed of straw. Rapid evaporation from the water surface and from the damp sides of the tray [due to the region's extremely low humidity] combined with the nocturnal drop in temperature to freeze the water—even though the temperature of the environment never fell near the freezing point." Pretty ingenious, huh? Perishable food was then placed on top of the ice that formed so that it would last at least a little bit longer.

Preheat the oven to 400 degrees.

Line a large, oiled, shallow casserole dish with half the potato, zucchini, and tomato, alternating slices of each to make a red, green, and white pattern. Sprinkle with half the cheese and herbs. Drizzle a little oil over it. Repeat one more layer, ending with cheese and herbs. Drizzle the chicken stock over the top. Bake for about 40 to 45 minutes, or until potatoes are tender. Cover with aluminum foil if top becomes too brown. Serves 6.

"The cherry tomato is a wonderful invention, producing, as it does, a satisfactorily explosive squish when bitten."
—Miss Manners

Enticing Entrées

The Marvelous Mainstay

Until she passed away at the age of 90 in 1995, **Hope Montgomery Scott** was the unofficial rip-roaring queen of Philadelphia high society. A bona fide party girl, Hope was the model for Katharine Hepburn's character in *The Philadelphia Story,* and entertained guests such as the Duke of Windsor (whom she once asked to reveal what was beneath his kilt—there is no record of his reply).

Perhaps the best anecdote about this grande dame concerns a dinner party she once hosted for fourteen friends. When a guest called shortly before the party to say he could not attend because he had a temperature of 104 degrees, Scott offered little in the way of sympathy. Upset that she would now have a seating of thirteen, which she thought to be unlucky, she probed to see if he, sick as he was, could somehow manage to sit up at her table. When he at last convinced her that he couldn't, she promptly replaced him with her dog. Did the dog manage to sit down for the entire dinner? That fact has been lost in the mists of time. But we bet if Hope had served any of the following meaty repasts, Fido would have been guaranteed to stay put.

In honor of this spicy socialite, we offer a very easy Jalapeño Pork Loin, which has been a hit at many Wild Woman dinner parties—it is *extremely* hot, but can be tamed.

Jalapeño Pork Loin and Potatoes

1 pork loin (about 1¼ pounds), cut in half lengthwise

⅛ cup chopped pickled jalapeños
(or diced mild green chilies, or a combination, depending on how spicy you like it)

½ cup reduced-calorie prepared Italian salad dressing

*½ 6-ounce can frozen orange juice concentrate,
thawed and undiluted*

*4 to 6 medium potatoes, chopped
(chop when ready to cook the roast)*

Sprinkle the inside of the loin with the peppers, tie back together with string, and place in a shallow baking dish. In a small bowl, combine the salad dressing and the orange juice concentrate and pour over the loin. Cover and refrigerate overnight, turning occasionally.

Preheat the oven to 350 degrees. Pour off about half of the marinade, then put the cut-up potatoes in the pan around the roast and stir to coat them. They must be in a single layer or they will not cook in time. Bake approximately one hour, basting frequently with the reserved marinade and turning the potatoes to brown evenly. Remove from the oven when a meat thermometer registers 170 degrees and the potatoes are done. Serves 4.

Clea's Flank Steak

¼ cup Worcestershire sauce

¼ cup lower-sodium soy sauce

3 tablespoons lemon juice

1 tablespoon minced fresh ginger

1 teaspoon freshly ground pepper

2 cloves garlic, pressed

1¼ pound flank steak

In a shallow dish big enough to hold the steak, whisk all ingredients except the steak. Add the steak and turn to coat, piercing all over with a fork. Cover and refrigerate overnight, turning occasionally.

Prepare a barbecue or preheat the broiler. Drain the marinade into a small saucepan and bring to a boil. Grill or broil the steak about 5 minutes per side for rare, 6 or 7 for more well done. Remove to a serving platter and thinly slice across the grain. Pass the marinade as a sauce. Serves 4.

————————  ————————

"Roast Beef, Medium, is not only a food. It is a philosophy."
—Edna Ferber

Never Interrupt Dinner

Nancy Hart was a Georgia housewife who, one day during the Revolutionary War, had dinner on the table for herself and her children when Royalist soldiers barged in. As they helped themselves to the food, she grabbed a gun, shot one, and held the rest at bay until help arrived. (The cads were hung; after all, they were exceedingly rude.) Hart's story inspired generations of feisty Georgian women. During the Civil War, the town of LaGrange, Georgia had the only female Confederate militia company—they called themselves the Nancy Harts.

Eleanor's Eggs

*I*n *Upstairs at the White House,* J.B. West describes **Eleanor Roosevelt's** Sunday evening salons. "The President did attend, if he felt well, and listened to the authors, artists, actresses, playwrights, sculptors, dancers, world travelers, old family friends—mixed in with ambassadors, Supreme Court justices, cabinet officers, and presidential advisors. Eleanor Roosevelt, using a large silver chafing dish she'd brought from Hyde Park, scrambled eggs at the table, but savored the conversation as the main course. She called the menu for the evening "scrambled eggs with brains."

Here, for a light supper, we offer a variation on scrambled eggs, but you will have to provide your own brains.

Chile Relleno Casserole

½ pound Monterey Jack cheese, shredded (may be lowfat)

½ pound Cheddar cheese, shredded (may be lowfat)

1 4-ounce can diced green chilies, mild or hot, drained

1 small onion, grated

4 large eggs, separated

⅓ cup milk (can be low- or nonfat)

1½ teaspoons flour

Salt and pepper to taste

1 large tomato, sliced

Salsa

Preheat the oven to 350 degrees. In a medium bowl, combine the cheeses, chilies, and onion; set aside.

Add the egg yolks and milk, flour, salt, and pepper. Stir well until the flour is all combined.

With an electric mixer on high, beat the egg whites in a medium bowl until they form stiff peaks. Gently fold them into the yolk mixture and fold half of this into the cheese mixture.

Spoon this into a buttered 8-inch-square casserole dish and spread the remaining egg mixture on top. Bake, uncovered, for 30 minutes. Arrange the tomato slices on top and bake another 15 minutes or until the eggs are firm. Let stand 5 minutes before serving. Serve with salsa. Serves 4.

———————— ⬮⬮ ————————

"Love and eggs should be fresh to be enjoyed."
—Russian proverb

Jessica Steams Up the Kitchen—
Well, Sometimes, Anyway

Well-known investigative journalist and certifiable wild woman **Jessica Mitford** (*The American Way of Death* is probably her best-known work) is a good friend of novelist Barbara Quick, who has placed pen to paper to give us the following perspective on this iconoclast.

Growing up among the British aristocracy as one of the six eccentric daughters of Lord and Lady Redesdale, Jessica Mitford was taught little in the way of domestic skills. Mitford describes, in her delightful memoir *Daughters and Rebels,* how her nanny was in agony when nineteen-year-old Jessica eloped with her cousin Esmond Romilly to fight with the Partisans in the Spanish civil war because "Little D," as she was called by her family, would have no one to wash her underclothes for her.

Many years later, after Romilly had died a hero's death fighting the Nazis, Jessica—known to all her friends as Decca—married labor lawyer and fellow lefty Robert Treuhaft, who was a crack household manager as well as an absolutely terrific cook. The famous muckraking journalist tells how once, when Bob was out of town, she decided to try her hand at some housework. She was halfway through sweeping the stairs when her daughter Dinky, then five or six, came up to her with a look of concern and said, "Aren't you supposed to start at the *top* of the stairs, Dec, and then work your way down?"

Son Benj came home from school one day soliciting a recipe from his mother for a cookbook being put together by Oakland, California public school boosters. Absorbed in whatever good fight she was waging at the time, Decca told Benj, "Well, I like roast duck. You can give them a recipe for that." "But they want to know how it's made," pleaded Benj. "Oh, I don't know," said Decca. "You take a duck and throw some oranges and things on top—I think you add some liquor—and then bake it for a while." Much to Benj's amusement or perhaps chagrin, while all the other mothers' recipes were conventional and detailed in their instructions, Decca's recipe for roast duck was printed exactly as she'd spoken it.

Bob Treuhaft came with the added bonus of a Hungarian-Jewish mother, Aranka, who was full of advice for Decca, including how to fire her husband up with ambition. "Tell him you want to be able to buy furs and jewels my dear. Let him apply himself with zeal." Decca complied by shouting out the window at Bob as he was leaving for the office, so that all the neighbors, but especially her mother-in-law, could hear her, "Get to work, you lazy, shiftless thing! I want furs! I want jewels!"

Not only did Aranka end up becoming Decca's staunch friend, but she also taught her brilliant daughter-in-law how to make Chicken Paprikas, a recipe that has been amended and even improved by Decca over the years:

Good!
October 98

Chicken Paprikas

2 tablespoons olive oil

2 tablespoons butter

2 large onions, chopped into bite-size pieces

2 large green peppers, chopped into bite-size pieces

1 4- to 5-pound chicken, cut up

Salt and pepper to taste

4 heaping tablespoons mild Hungarian paprika

4 heaping tablespoons tomato paste

2 cloves of garlic, crushed

In a Dutch oven over medium-high heat, heat the oil and butter. Add the onions and green pepper and sauté lightly. Arrange half the chicken pieces on top of the onions. Add salt and pepper, plus half the paprika, tomato paste, and garlic. Place the rest of the chicken on top, then the remaining paprika, tomato paste, and garlic. Cover and cook slowly on top of the stove until chicken is tender, about 1 hour or so. Turn the chicken pieces a few times during cooking. Serves 4.

Women Writers Steam Up the Kitchen

- Jeannette Winterson: *Oranges Are Not the Only Fruit*
- Banana Yoshimoto: *Kitchen*
- Anne Tyler: the turkey scene in *The Accidental Tourist*
- Laura Esquivel: *Like Water for Chocolate*
- Amy Tan: *The Kitchen God's Wife, The Joy Luck Club, The Hundred Secret Senses*
- Fannie Flagg: *Fried Green Tomatoes at the Whistle Stop Cafe*
- Margaret Visser: *Much Depends on Dinner, The Rituals of Dinner*

Catherine de Medici's Dowry

*T*he habits of queens can affect an entire cuisine. A case in point: In 1533 **Catherine de Medici** of Florence (yes, from *that* scheming, poisoning, and conspiring family) was betrothed to the Dauphin of France, who was soon to become King Henri II. (By the way, Catherine was orphaned at birth. Reflecting the dangers of the time, her mother Madeleine had died at age seventeen, shortly after giving birth to Catherine, while her father, Lorenzo, died two weeks later at age twenty-seven of syphilis and tuberculosis.)

Catherine's marriage, like those of many other Medicis, was arranged to cement relations with the French aristocracy, and she brought with her not only the requisite number of ladies-in-waiting but her own chefs and pastry cooks too. Later that century, Marie de Medici imported even more Italian cooks when she became bride to France's Henri IV, including confectioner Giovanni Pastilla,

who was responsible for inventing pastilles. (His candies were so popular with the royal children that they coined the term *bonbon*, literally "good-good," still in use today.) Between them, the two queens were responsible for introducing a whole new Italian style of cooking to France, and from then on, the French never looked back.

Here's how at least one entrée made the journey. As Catherine was packing her bags for the voyage to Marseille (well, no, of course she didn't actually pack them herself), a quick-thinking cleric, remembering that the way to a man's heart is through his

stomach, persuaded the Medici family to add a bag of *fagioli* to the future princess's dowry, tucked among the pearls and lace. Thus was born the famous bean dish of France, *cassoulet*. But Catherine did not stop there, for she is also credited with bringing peas, sorbet, and most importantly, the recipe for that other most Gallic of entrées, Canard à l'Orange.

And while she must have made her husband—and by extension the rest of the royal family—culinarily happy, eventually cassoulet came to be considered "peasant food," perhaps because it is a one-pot meal. Here we present a vegetarian cassoulet, which no doubt would have shocked the likes of the Medicis. It is time-consuming to make, although you can streamline the process a bit if you soak the beans overnight. Naturally, we also offer a Duck with Orange Sauce for your dining pleasure.

Vegetarian Cassoulet

1 pound dried Great Northern beans

3 tablespoons olive oil

2 heads garlic, cloves separated and peeled, but left whole

2 medium-sized potatoes, peeled and diced

1 red bell pepper, diced

1 carrot, diced

1 teaspoon "herbes de Provence"

¼ teaspoon dried thyme

Salt and pepper

1½ cups dry red wine

2 cups diced tomatoes

1½ cups vegetable broth

1 pickled jalapeño (en escabeche), chopped

1 cup bread crumbs

3 to 4 tablespoons chopped fresh parsley

Onion-Jalapeño Relish

1 onion, chopped

2 garlic cloves, chopped

3 to 4 pickled jalapeños (en escabeche), chopped

Juice of 1 lemon

Spoonful of jalapeño brine

Pick over the beans for any bits of grit or stone, then place in a heavy saucepan and cover with water. Bring to a boil, cook 1 or 2 minutes, cover, and remove from the heat. Let sit at least 1 hour, then drain and add fresh water to cover. Bring to a boil, reduce heat, and slowly simmer, partially covered, until the beans are tender, 1 to 2 hours. Drain and set aside.

In sauté pan, heat the olive oil. Add all but four garlic cloves, the potatoes, red pepper, and carrot; lightly sauté for 5 minutes.

Preheat the oven to 350 degrees. Layer the drained beans with the sautéed vegetables in a Dutch oven, sprinkling with "herbes de Provence," thyme, salt, and pepper as you go. Top with the red wine, tomatoes, broth, and jalapeño. Cover and bake for about 1½ hours, checking every so often to

be sure the mixture is not too dry. Add more broth if needed to keep the mixture slightly soupy.

Chop the reserved garlic and combine with the bread crumbs and parsley. Uncover and spread the bread crumb mixture over the cassoulet. Increase the temperature to 400 degrees, and bake for 15 minutes, until the crust is golden brown.

Make the Onion-Jalapeño Relish by combining all ingredients. Serve the casserole, accompanied by the relish. Serves 4.

Duck à l'Orange

1 duckling, no larger than 4 pounds

2 oranges

1 tablespoon butter

3 tablespoons olive oil

1 carrot, coarsely chopped

1 medium onion, sliced

1 bouquet garni of parsley, thyme, and bay leaf

¾ cup white wine

2 cups chicken stock

½ lemon

Orange Sauce

2 tablespoons sugar

2 tablespoons cider vinegar

2 tablespoons curaçao or Grand Marnier (optional)

1 tablespoon arrowroot (optional)

Preheat the oven to 350 degrees. Remove any giblets from the duck cavity and rinse the duck. Cut one orange into quarters and stuff into the cavity; truss the duckling like a turkey. In the bottom of an ovenproof casserole over a medium-high flame, melt the butter and oil. Add the duckling and brown very lightly on all sides. Add the carrot, onion, bouquet garni, and white wine. Cover, bring to a boil over medium heat, and reduce the wine to half the amount. Add the stock, bring back to a boil, and then place in the oven for 60 to 90 minutes or until the juices run clear.

Meanwhile, remove the rind from the remaining orange and lemon half; blanch, drain, and cut into julienne strips. Set aside. When the duck is done, transfer it to a serving plate, remove the trussing and oranges, and keep warm while making Orange Sauce.

To make the sauce, strain and degrease the liquid remaining in the roasting pan and set aside. In a small bowl, combine the Grand Marnier with the arrowroot if desired. Set aside.

In a small saucepan over moderately high heat, boil the sugar and vinegar for several minutes until the mixture caramelizes into a mahogany-brown syrup. Immediately remove from heat and add half of the cooking liquid. Simmer for 1 minute to dissolve the caramel, stirring occasionally. Then add the rest of the cooking liquid and arrowroot mixture if desired, and boil down until thick.

Add the reserved julienned rind, pour the sauce over the duckling, and serve immediately. Serves 4.

She Took Them to Her Grave

Soybeans have long been considered a staple of the impover-ished, but, according to Reay Tannahill in *Food in History,* "the dis-covery of a bamboo slip mentioning soy sauce and fermented black bean sauce in the tomb of a wife of the first Marquis of Tai indicates that the soy bean was becoming upwardly mobile in 160 B.C. Now a staple of Chinese cooking, the soybean may have an even more auspicious future—as the fuel for a Chinese economy car now in development."

Of Erudite Princesses and Frightening Forks

Around 1000 A.D., while touring the Middle East, a wealthy nobleman from Venice met a beautiful Turkish princess. They fell in love, married, and decided to set up housekeeping in Venice. Along with her clothes and jewels, the princess brought to her new home a case of forks. Forks had been in common use in the royal courts of the Middle East since at least the seventh century, and the princess had used them all her life.

However, the princess's forks created quite a stir when she set them out for her first dinner party. One observer explained, "Instead of eating with her fingers like other people, the princess cuts up her food into small pieces and eats them by means of little golden forks with two prongs." Another declared her behavior "luxurious beyond belief."

The conservative Venetian church fathers were outraged. "God in his wisdom has provided man with natural forks—his fingers," said one. (Sound familiar?) "Therefore it is an insult to Him to substitute artificial metallic forks for them when eating."

Soon after the fork debut, the princess came down with a dreadful illness and died. The will of God, some proclaimed; others believed it was due to the filthy habit of eating with a fork. Either way, it would be another three hundred years before fork use became common in Italy.

It took even longer to catch on in the rest of Europe. When Catherine de Medici went to France to marry the king in 1533, she too brought her forks, but the French were resistant to their charms. Nor were they popular in England even seventy years later, when the traveler Tom Coryqt flattered himself that he

had introduced the utensil. (Once again, feminine achievements being usurped by men!) Indeed, until well into the eighteenth century most north Europeans continued to eschew fork use. "Even as late as 1897," writes Reay Tannahill in *Food in History,* "the British Navy was forbidden the use of knives and forks, which were considered prejudicial to discipline and manliness."

Not being too worried about our manliness, since the Turkish princess and Catherine de Medici made it possible for us to keep our fingers clean when we eat, we present two very marvelous and messy fork-dependent dishes in honor of this achievement.

Artichoke Heart and Roasted Garlic Timbale with Roasted Red Pepper Purée

(Nicole Alper)

3 cups cooked artichoke hearts

6 eggs

⅔ cup Jarlsberg cheese, grated

⅔ cup heavy cream

¼ cup roasted garlic purée

1 teaspoon salt

1 teaspoon pepper

⅔ cup bread crumbs (from fresh white bread)

Roasted Red Pepper Purée

4 large red peppers

1 tablespoon balsamic vinegar

½ cup chicken stock

Salt and pepper to taste

Chopped fresh parsley for garnish

In a food processor purée half of the artichoke hearts. Add the other half and pulse for only a few seconds, so that there are still small pieces of the artichoke in the mixture. Transfer to a bowl and mix in first the eggs, then the rest of the ingredients (except for Roasted Red Pepper Purée). Season to taste. Pour into a well-greased soufflé dish. Bake in a preheated 350-degree oven for 5 minutes, then lower to 325 and continue baking for 25 to 30 minutes or until the timbale is set.

While the timbale is baking, make the Red Pepper Purée. Place the washed peppers directly on individual burners, leaving the skin on, and slowly roast over a low flame. Turn them frequently with tongs. When the skins are completely black, remove the peppers from the heat and place in a bowl of cold water. Cover and let sit for a few minutes. Then, one at a time, begin peeling off the black outer layer. Slice open the peppers and remove the seeds; then put into a food processor along with the other ingredients. Purée. Season to taste with salt and pepper.

When the timbale is cooked, trace around the inside of the dish with a knife, to loosen it from the sides. Cover with a large plate and turn over. Shake gently to remove the timbale. Pour some sauce around the base of the timbale, covering the bottom of the plate. Garnish with the chopped parsley. Serves 6.

Chicken Pot-au-Feu

2 teaspoons olive oil

1 chicken, about 3 pounds, cut into serving pieces

6 cups chicken broth

1 teaspoon coriander seeds, crushed

2 cloves garlic, peeled and thinly sliced

1 medium-size onion, peeled and quartered

4 small carrots, peeled and cut into 2-inch lengths

8 small new potatoes, halved

*4 leeks, white and light green parts only, washed
and cut into 2-inch pieces*

Salt and pepper to taste

2 teaspoons chopped fresh Italian parsley

In a large, wide pot over medium-high heat, heat the olive oil. Add the chicken and sear until browned, about 4 minutes per side. Remove from the pot and set aside. Place the chicken broth, coriander seeds, and garlic in the pot and bring to a boil. Add the chicken, lower the heat, partially cover, and simmer for 20 minutes.

Add the remaining ingredients, partially cover, and simmer until the chicken and vegetables are tender, about 30 minutes. Divide the chicken and vegetables among 4 large bowls and ladle the broth over them. Serves 4.

No Cowering for This Queen of Cows

The largest cattle ranch in the world was started by a woman, **Henrietta Chamberlain King**, in 1886, when she inherited a debt-ridden six hundred thousand Texas acres from her deceased husband. Running the spread with her son-in-law, she pioneered some of the earliest scientific techniques for beef production, including the development of hardy Santa Gertrudis cattle (a cross between a shorthorn and a Brahma), for which King Ranch is now renowned. An extremely shrewd businesswoman, she also induced a railroad to build through her property (thus eliminating the problem of getting the cattle to the slaughterhouses) and solved the problem of water (always an issue in the American West) by importing a new kind of well-drilling rig that tapped an artesian well. When she died in 1925 at the age of ninety-two, the ranch consisted of one million acres and she left an estate worth over $5 million. Today, the King Ranch has holdings not only in Texas, but in Brazil, Argentina, Venezuela, and Australia.

For this accomplishment, we *must* of course present a Texas beef recipe or two.

Texas Carne Asada

1 beef skirt steak, 1 to 1½ pounds

Juice of 3 limes

¼ cup tequila

6 cloves garlic, chopped

2 serrano chilies, thinly sliced

¼ *cup cilantro, finely chopped*

1 teaspoon salt

Flour tortillas

Salsa of your choice

Guacamole

In a pan big enough to hold the steak in one layer, combine the lime juice, tequila, garlic, serranos, cilantro, and salt. Add the steak and turn to coat with marinade. Cover tightly and let marinate in the refrigerator overnight, turning at least once.

Discard the marinade. Grill the meat over hot coals 3 to 4 minutes per side. Slice thinly across the grain. Serve with tortillas, salsa, and guacamole for each person to assemble as desired. Serves 4.

Texas Chili

2 cups beef broth

3 New Mexico chiles

3 ancho chiles

3 tablespoons oil

3 pounds beef chuck, cut into ½-inch cubes

¼ *pound smoked bacon, diced*

2 onions, chopped

6 cloves garlic, chopped

2 tablespoons cumin

1 tablespoon oregano leaves

½ teaspoon cinnamon

5 serrano chiles, thinly sliced

2 16-ounce cans tomato sauce

3½ to 4 cups chopped tomatoes

2 cups beer

½ cup brown sugar

Salt and cayenne pepper to taste

4 cups cooked pinto or red kidney beans
(canned is fine)

Garnishes:

Salsa of choice

1 onion, chopped

5 to 10 pickled jalapeños

1 cup shredded Cheddar cheese

2 cups shredded lettuce

2 cups sour cream

Heat the broth to boiling and pour it over the New Mexico and ancho chiles. Cover and let stand for 1 hour. Remove stems, tear chiles into 1-inch pieces, and purée in a blender or processor to a smooth paste, adding broth gradually to make a sauce. Use the remaining broth in chili. Set the chile purée aside.

Heat the oil and brown the beef. Add the bacon, onions, garlic, and spices, and cook until the onion is translucent. Add the chile purée, serranos, reserved broth, tomato sauce, tomatoes, beer, and brown sugar. Simmer uncovered for 1½ to 2 hours, then taste for seasoning. Add salt and cayenne to taste. Serve alongside the beans and garnishes so that each diner can "dress" her or his own. Serves 8.

These Dames Give Fast Food a Good Name

Who invented chili is a matter of hot dispute. However, by the 1880s "chili queens" roamed the streets of San Antonio selling their wares from bubbling cauldrons set in carts. "Each chili queen had a big, ornate lamp," writes Frank Tolbert in *A Bowl of Red,* "often an antique, with globes of red, yellow, orange, or some other vivid color to catch the eyes of customers, who had already been hooked by the chili scent." The women dressed in bright colors, with roses pinned to their bosoms, and were accompanied by street musicians, who would serenade the diners as they wolfed down the spicy mix.

"Approach love like a bowl of chili: the hotter the better."
—Gladiolia Montana & Texas Bix Bender

Tireless Tillie's Time-Saving Tomatoes

Henrietta King is not the only feisty farming female around. Take New York divorcée **Myrtle "Tillie" Ehrlich**. In 1934, she got it in her mind to produce Italian canning tomatoes, but was advised by the U.S. Department of Agriculture that they couldn't be grown in the U.S. Convinced that the Feds were wrong, Tillie took her savings and sailed for Italy where, on the ship, she met Italian pomodoro canner Florindo Del Gaizo. (We know—it sounds just like a movie from the thirties, but honest, it happened this way!) Tillie convinced Del Gaizo that tomatoes could indeed be grown in California, and he loaned her $10,000 to get started. She then persuaded the Pacific Can Company in Stockton, California to build a canning factory for her to rent, and Tillie Lewis Foods of California was off and running. Thirteen years later, Tillie decides to remarry and sells out to a conglomerate for $6 million. Now that's a lot of tomatoes!

Obviously Tillie was one astute businesswoman—and she must have been handy in the kitchen too, for any good cook knows that the one processed item worth keeping in stock is canned tomatoes. With a supply of ready-cuts on hand, plus an onion and a clove of garlic, you can whip up a luscious pasta sauce faster than you can say Chef Boyardee™. Here are two of our favorites. The first literally takes no more than 15 minutes.

"Everything you see I owe to spaghetti."
—Sophia Loren

Linguine with Tuna, Black Olives, and Tomatoes

1 4½-ounce can tomatoes

1 1-pound package linguine

2 tablespoons olive oil

1 garlic clove, pressed

1 6½-ounce can tuna in water, drained and flaked

3 tablespoons pitted and chopped Kalamata olives

2 tablespoons chopped fresh parsley

Drain the tomatoes, reserving the liquid, and chop if whole.

Cook the linguine according to package directions. As the water is coming to a boil, heat the oil in a medium skillet and add the garlic; sauté for 1 minute. Add the remaining ingredients and sauté, stirring occasionally, for 5 minutes. Add some reserved tomato juice if it seems too dry. Serves 4.

Angel Hair Pasta with Artichoke and Tomato Sauce

1 6-ounce jar marinated artichoke hearts

1 large onion, chopped

4 cloves garlic, pressed

Splash of red wine (optional)

2 14½-ounce cans tomatoes, broken up if not already cut

½ cup chopped fresh basil

3 tablespoons chopped roasted red peppers

1 1-pound package angel hair pasta

Remove the artichokes from the jar, reserving the marinade, and chop into small pieces. Set aside.

Pour the marinade into a medium saucepan over medium-high heat and sauté the onions and garlic until limp. Add a splash of red wine, if desired, and allow the sauce to reduce a bit. Add the tomatoes and basil and allow to simmer until thickened, about 1 hour. (If time is of the essence, add a bit of tomato paste—1 to 2 tablespoons—to thicken quicker.)

When the sauce is of desired consistency, prepare the pasta according to package directions. While the pasta is cooking, add the reserved artichoke hearts and the red peppers to the sauce until just heated through. Serves 4.

"Tomatoes and oregano make it Italian; wine and tarragon make it French.
Sour cream makes it Russian; lemon and cinnamon make it Greek.
Soy sauce makes it Chinese; garlic makes it good."
—Alice May Brock

Rock and Roll Women

Belinda Carlisle was the lead singer of the 1980s band the Go-Go's, the first female band to earn the number one spot on the Billboard charts for both a single, "Our Lips Are Sealed," and an album, *Beauty and the Beat.* Carlisle was a Los Angeles high school cheerleader who haunted punk clubs on weekends and, with a friend, was inspired to start her own band after seeing the Sex Pistols' final performance. Laughed at initially ("When we first had rehearsals, [the other women] didn't even know how to plug in their equipment," explained guitarist Charlotte Caffey), they went on to great success—*Beauty and the Beat* sold over two million copies—but took a lot of heat from the music press, who continued to criticize their musical abilities, and from feminists who were angry with their provocative presentation of themselves. Ultimately the group crashed and burned in the typical rock combo of drugs, alcohol, egos, and money disputes. Ironically, the success of the Go-Go's did not open up the field for female performers, according to *She's a Rebel, The History of Women in Rock and Roll,* but in "some ways narrowed the field: all-female bands who emerged in the wake of the Go-Go's . . . automatically ended up being compared to them, even if it was only to say that despite the fact that Band X was composed entirely of women, they still sounded nothing like America's Number One All-Female Band."

Not surprisingly for a rocker who knows how to pour on the heat, Belinda's entrée featured here is a spicy one. She claims her cauliflower curry "is not for the timid of tongue." We suggest you modify it for your own taste buds and serve it over rice for a vegetarian entrée.

Hot and Spicy Cauliflower a Go Go

(from *The Rock and Roll Cookbook*)

½ cup olive oil

⅓ cup fresh ginger, chopped and peeled

1 bulb garlic, cloves peeled, but left whole

1 heaping teaspoon each turmeric, Garam Masala
(available at Indian groceries and specialty food
stores), curry powder, and crushed red chilies

1 teaspoon salt

2 jalapeño chilies, cut into quarters

2 to 3 tomatoes, peeled and cut into quarters

2 medium cauliflowers, cut into large bite-sized pieces

In a large skillet over a medium-high flame, heat the olive oil. Add the ginger root and sauté 3 to 4 minutes. Add whole peeled garlic cloves and cook 2 more minutes, stirring constantly. Add the spices and chilies, then the tomatoes and cauliflower pieces. Lower the heat to medium and cook, stirring occasionally, until the tomatoes are saucy and the cauliflower can easily be pierced with a fork. Serves 4.

"I know I have the body of a weak and feeble woman,
but I have the heart and stomach of a King,
and a King of England, too."
—Elizabeth I, "Good Queen Beth," in a 1588 speech to her troops
upon the approach of the Spanish armada

Songs for a Wild Kitchen

Singles:

Butter Ball

Buttered Popcorn

Drinkin' Wine Spo-Dee-O Dee

Hot Pastrami

Hot Stuff

Lady Marmalade

Lemon Tree

Lollipop

Mashed Potato Time

Rock Lobster

Salt Peanuts

Soul Kitchen

Steam Heat

A Taste of Honey

Tutti Frutti

Vanilla O'Lay

Waitress

While You're Out Looking
   for Sugar

Albums:

A Salt with a Deadly Pepa

Eat to the Beat

A Lonely Grain of Corn

Milk and Honey

More Songs About Buildings
   and Food

Pressure Cookin'

Raw Like Sushi

Take a Bite

Surreal Supper

ormerly a prostitute, **Kiki** (one of the first mono-named glamour gals) gained fame as an artist's model in the Parisian Left Bank during the 1920s. The lover and muse of surrealist artist Man Ray, her face and body appeared in many of his paintings and photographs, including the famous photograph with a violin superimposed on her back.

Surrealism was a literary, artistic, and philosophical movement that sought to suspend conscious reason, aesthetics, and morality to allow for the expression of subconscious thought and feeling. Surrealists did not just produce disruptive art; they believed it was important to live outside the normal constraints of middle-class life. Despite such Bohemian credentials, our two lovebirds actually lived a quietly domestic life. When not posing for posterity, Kiki could be found in the kitchen, cooking up Boeuf Bourguignonne for Man and his pals.

Boeuf Bourguignonne

2½ pounds beef chuck, cut into large cubes

All-purpose flour

3 tablespoons olive oil

Salt and pepper to taste

⅛ cup cognac, optional

¼ pound bacon, diced

2 cloves garlic, chopped

1 carrot, coarsely chopped

1 leek, well washed and coarsely chopped

1 large onion, coarsely chopped

1 bay leaf

1 teaspoon dried thyme

1 tablespoon chopped fresh parsley

½ bottle burgundy or other red wine

2 tablespoons butter

18 whole pearl onions, peeled

18 whole mushroom caps, washed

Roll the beef in the flour. Over a high flame, heat the oil, add the beef, and brown on all sides. Sprinkle with salt and pepper, pour on the cognac, and ignite. When the flame dies out, transfer the meat to an ovenproof 2-quart casserole dish. Preheat the oven to 350 degrees.

Put the skillet back on medium high and add the bacon, garlic, carrots, leeks, and chopped onions. Cook, stirring, until bacon is crispy and vegetables are light brown, then add to the casserole. Add the bay leaf, thyme, parsley, wine, and, if necessary, enough water to barely cover the meat. Cover and bake 2 hours.

Make a paste of 1 tablespoon butter and 1 tablespoon flour and stir bit by bit into the casserole. Add the whole onions and continue cooking 1½ more hours, or until the meat is tender. Just before serving, melt the remaining butter in the skillet and sauté the mushrooms until light brown. Take the casserole out, stir in the mushrooms, and serve. Serves 4.

And Then There's the *Real* French Chef

Boeuf Bourguignonne has a proud association with wild women in the kitchen. One of the most riotous chefs of all, Julia Child, launched her first PBS cooking show in 1964 with her version of the French classic. Julia had studied at Le Cordon Bleu in Paris and started a French food craze in the U.S. in the sixties with her bestselling cookbook, *Mastering the Art of French Cooking* (which she penned with two French women, Louisette Bertholle and Simone Beck). (The three also started a French cooking school for Americans in Paris, L'Ecole des Troise Gourmandes.) Julia's popularity led to her own TV show, which subsequently spawned dozens of others.

Known for her high-pitched voice and her zany, uninhibited style—once, gazing at something she had just prepared, she opined, "It is so beautifully arranged on the plate—you know someone's fingers have been all over it"—the indefatigable Child has been at the forefront of the "gourmandization" of Americans. Besides cooking schools, cookbooks, and TV shows, she has done cooking CD-ROMs, was an early endorser of the Cuisinart, and is one of the founders of the International Institute of Food and Wine. Julia's iconoclastic style is perhaps best illustrated by the following. Once, while filming her show—back then it was live, not taped—Julia dropped a cooked chicken on the floor. Quickly, she put it back on the plate, began garnishing, and said, "Remember, you are alone in the kitchen."

Love Me Crunchy, Love Me Do

h the trials and tribulations of being married to a living legend! In her autobiography, *Elvis & Me*, **Priscilla Presley** bemoans being in charge of the King's chow. "Every night before dinner was served, I came downstairs first, checked with the maids to see that his food was just the way he like it—his mashed potatoes creamily whipped, plenty of cornbread, and his meat burned to perfection."

It was a good thing they could afford a chef, because apparently Elvis found cooking beneath him and Priscilla didn't know a soup pot from a soufflé dish. Fortunately Elvis loved her anyway, as this story demonstrates. "I decided one evening to show off my cooking skills for everyone by making one of Elvis' favorite dishes, lasagna... I tried to appear cool and confident as I brought out the fancily prepared platter and started cutting individual squares for my guests. I did notice that when I started slicing the lasagna, it felt a little tough, but thinking I was holding a dull knife, I continued dishing it out.

"I sat down, smiled anxiously, and said, 'Please start. We all took a bite and—crunch. There was a look of shock on everyone's face. I looked at my plate and was mortified when I realized I had forgotten to boil the pasta.

"Elvis began laughing, but when he saw I was about to cry he turned to his plate and began eating, uncooked noodles and all. Taking their lead from him, everyone followed suit."

Times have changed since Priscilla's culinary calamity—specifically, the microwave oven has been invented. And that spells good new for P.P. and for all of us because now it is possible to assemble lasagna with uncooked noodles. You can do it with any recipe using 3½ cups sauce for a 2- or 3-quart baking pan. Just assemble as usual—but don't cook the noodles—then cover with vented plastic wrap and cook on high for 6 minutes, then on medium high for 20 minutes or until noodles are tender.

If you're not the trusting type, or have sworn off microwaves, here's a stellar lasagna offered with standard cooking instructions. Your choice—oven or microwave.

Great!
June 98

Ricotta, Tomato, and Spinach Noodle Lasagna

3 tablespoons olive oil

1 garlic clove, crushed

1 28-ounce can tomatoes with juices, crushed

salt and pepper

16 spinach lasagna noodles

*1 15-ounce container ricotta cheese
(can be lowfat)*

¼ cup grated Parmesan cheese

1 egg, beaten

Pinch of ground nutmeg

*1 pound mozzarella cheese, coarsely shredded
(can be lowfat)*

½ cup loosely packed torn fresh basil leaves

In a medium skillet, heat the oil; add the garlic and sauté until golden. Add the tomatoes and heat to simmering. Cook, stirring, over medium heat until the sauce is thickened and reduced, about 20 minutes. Season with salt and pepper to taste.

Cook the lasagna noodles in plenty of boiling salted water until al dente, or firm to the bite, about 12 minutes; drain. Let the noodles sit in a bowl of cool water until ready to use. Combine the ricotta, Parmesan, egg, and nutmeg; whisk to blend.

Preheat the oven to 350 degrees. Spoon just enough of the tomato sauce into a 9x13x2-inch baking dish to lightly coat the bottom. Lift the lasagna noodles individually from the water and blot dry on paper towels. Arrange a layer of 4 slightly overlapping lasagna noodles on the bottom of the dish. Top with a quarter of the ricotta and mozzarella. Spoon a quarter of the tomato sauce over the first layer of noodles; sprinkle with a few basil leaves. Repeat until you have used up all ingredients, ending with a layer of sauce.

Bake 45 minutes. Let stand 15 minutes before serving. Serves 6.

The largest lasagna ever made in the U.S. weighed 3,477 pounds and measured 63 feet by 7 feet. It was made by the sororities and fraternities of Cornell University in October 1991.

The Dueling Doyennes of Dieting

What is it about women and diets? Not only do we go on them, but in the past thirty years a number of determined dieters of the female persuasion have decided to get out of the kitchen and into the diet industry, a business that is potentially lucrative (over $30 billion is spent yearly in the United States on diet-related products), if volatile (weight loss fads come and go in the blink of an eye). "Former fat" women who have at one time been associated with diet franchises are Sybil Ferguson, who lost fifty-eight pounds and founded The Diet Center; Lois Lindauer, who shed forty-two pounds and began the Diet Workshop; and Jenny Craig (number of pounds lost after pregnancy not revealed) of the Jenny Craig Weight Loss Centers.

But the most famous of these is one-time compulsive eater Jean Nidetch of Queens, New York, who founded Weight Watchers International, the most successful diet enterprise to date, in 1964. The idea for the company grew out of Jean's own loss of seventy-two pounds by meeting with a group of friends who encouraged each other in their efforts to stick to a medically recommended diet. She realized that no matter the diet, without support and peer pressure, the weight will come back. So she designed a comprehensive program of diet, education, group support, and weekly "weigh-ins" that eventually grew into a worldwide operation with an average weekly attendance of half a million. Jean no longer rules the roost; in 1983 she sold out, for an undisclosed sum, to Heinz (of ketchup fame). Heinz has built a Weight Watchers empire that now includes a magazine and several cookbooks, frozen diet dinners and soft drinks on sale in supermarkets, and summer camps for overweight teenagers; there's even talk of a chain of Weight Watchers restaurants.

The latest ladies to hit it big in dieting circles are, of course, **Rosie Daley**, the woman who helped Oprah slim down (and subsequently sold a million-plus copies of her lowfat cookbook), and cable TV diet guru **Susan Powter**. Which only proves that as long as women continue to strive to be thin, there will be an insatiable hunger for diets. Here's a mouthwatering recipe with only ninety-six calories in honor of all these slimming women—and it only takes twenty minutes from start to finish.

Soy Baked Fish

1 tablespoon lower-sodium soy sauce

1 teaspoon grated fresh ginger

1 garlic clove, chopped

½ cup chicken or vegetable broth

1 teaspoon sugar

4 fish fillets, about 3 ounces each
(can be snapper, halibut, or any white-fleshed fish)

"Women should try to increase their size rather than decrease it,
because I believe the bigger we are, the more space we'll
take up, and the more we'll have to be reckoned with.
I think every woman should be fat like me."

—Roseanne, in her pre-dieting and plastic surgery days

Preheat the oven to 450 degrees. In a shallow casserole dish, combine the soy sauce, ginger, garlic, broth, and sugar. Place the fish in pan in a single layer. Let marinate for a few minutes, turn over, and let marinate for another few minutes.

Bake, basting a few times with the sauce, until the fish is opaque, about 10 minutes. Serve with the sauce. Serves 4.

Blame It on Lulu

American women's obsession with thinness was ushered in in 1924 by the book *Diet and Health* by Lulu Hunt Peters, M.D., which remained on the bestseller list for five years. The "Siren of Slenderizing", "as she was called, had American women, striving for the flapper's boyish slimness, endlessly counting calories and measuring their waistlines," writes Charles Panati in *Panati's Parade of Fads, Follies, and Manias*. Dr. Peters, who waged a lifelong battle with the scales herself, also had her own newspaper column in which she offered such comments as, "How you hate it [being fat]. But cheer up! I will save you as I have saved myself and many, many others!" Actually, despite such evangelical diatribes, she was on the right track: she encouraged people to exercise, was one of the first doctors to talk about the dangers of fatty foods, and believed in a diet of whole grains and fresh fruits and vegetables.

Summing up her life, she exclaimed, "It is not in vain that all my life I have had to fight the too, too solid."

She's Hogtied—And Loving It

Dee Van De Walle loves pigs. A licensed artificial inseminator who also serves as a "midwife" to the hogs she raises, Iowan Dee Van De Walle was, in 1974, the first woman ever to win the Iowa Master Pork Producers Award. The author of a newspaper column called "Let's Talk Pork," she also produced a slide show that demonstrates her own swine-raising operation, and participated in a City-Farm Swap sponsored by the Agriculture Council of America, in which she played hostess to a family from Chicago who visited her farm to become acquainted with rural lifestyles. What would Dee have served for dinner? Smothered Pork Chops, we presume, a recipe straight from the heartland. We also offer another pork recipe whose influences are found in other parts of the world.

Good May 99

Smothered Pork Chops

1 tablespoon brown sugar

Salt and pepper to taste

6 ¾-inch-thick pork chops

All-purpose flour

2 tablespoons vegetable oil

1 medium onion, thinly sliced

1 medium green pepper, thinly sliced

1 lemon, sliced and seeded

"America's Greatest Pig Woman"

That's what Betty Shingler Talmadge's employees engraved on a gold pig they once presented her as a token of their esteem. Maybe so. For thirty-five years, Betty was the loyal wife of Herman E. Talmadge, the senator from Georgia. To distract herself from her husband's roving eye and heavy drinking, Betty parlayed a small ham business into a three-and-a-half-million-dollar corporation that she sold in 1969; later she began a meat brokerage business and published a cookbook entitled *How to Cook a Pig and Other Back-to-the-Farm Recipes.* Then, one day in 1977, she heard on TV that her husband was suing her for divorce. Embroiled in a fierce property suit with her ex (on whom sanctions were later imposed by the Senate for financial mismanagement), she decided to run for Congress while he was still in the Senate—an unheard-of event at the time. Explaining to the *New York Times* in 1978 that "The thing that has saved me [in the divorce] is good friends and work," she urged women "to have something of their own to fall back on . . . I've been in business twenty-six years . . . There's not much difference between selling a ham and selling a political idea." In the same article, the *Times* reporter noted that Betty had needlepointed a chair in her library which read, "Uppity Women Unite." Unfortunately, Betty lost in the primary and her opponent went on to be beaten by Newt Gingrich.

Combine the sugar, salt, and pepper; rub this mixture on both sides of the pork chops and then coat the chops well with flour.

In a large deep skillet, heat the oil and fry the chops until browned on both sides; remove from the skillet and set aside.

Add the onion and green pepper to the skillet; sauté until just tender, then return the chops to the skillet. Add the lemon slices and about ½ inch of water. Cover and simmer over low heat 1 hour or until very tender, adding additional water if necessary. Serves 6.

Pork Fajitas

1 pound lean boneless pork

2 cloves garlic, minced

1 teaspoon dried oregano, crumbled

½ teaspoon dried cumin

1 teaspoon seasoned salt

2 tablespoons orange juice

2 tablespoons vinegar

Dash of hot pepper sauce

1 tablespoon cooking oil

1 medium onion, peeled and sliced

1 green pepper, seeded and sliced

Flour tortillas

Green onion tops, sliced

Shredded lettuce

Bottled salsa

Slice the pork across the grain into ⅛-inch strips. In a bowl big enough to hold the pork strips, combine the garlic, oregano, cumin, salt, orange juice, vinegar, and hot pepper. Add the pork and marinate for 15 minutes, stirring occasionally. Stir-fry until the pork is no longer pink, about 3 to 5 minutes. Serve with the flour tortillas, sliced green onion, shredded lettuce, and salsa so diners can assemble their own fajitas. Serves 4.

Kitchen Strike Gets Results

Louisiana was settled by Frenchmen in the late 1600s and early 1700s. Tired of the absence from female companionship they petitioned the Bishop of Quebec to send some young women to the colony. In 1727, a boatload of girls arrived in the care of Ursuline nuns, with whom they stayed until marriage. Known as "casket girls" for the casket of clothes they brought with them, they soon expressed dissatisfaction with their new home. It wasn't the weather or even the men, but the food. After eating nothing but cornmeal for several weeks, they marched to the governor and declared that they didn't care for this native flour in any form—white, yellow, or blue—and they would not cook until they could use French wheat flour. Unfortunately, wheat flour was not to be had in any quantity, but the conflict was resolved when the governor's cook, Madame Langlois, taught the girls the cooking secrets she learned from the Choctaw Indians—adding wild honey to corn bread, how to prepare whole hominy and grits, and the stuffing of squirrel, hare, duck, and turkey.

Female Ingenuity

reland has never been known as the land of plenty, and during hard times, Irish mothers used to stretch the family meal of potatoes by serving "fish-and-point." "This apocryphal recipe," reports Jeremy MacClancy in *Consuming Culture,* "consists of a large serving dish with a herring painted on it and a pyramid of salt in its center. Each diner forks one of the potatoes on his [sic] plate, dips it in the salt, and points it at a section of the fish, crying, 'That's my bit!' On eating the potato he then exclaims, 'Hmm! How good the fish tastes. Perfectly cooked! It's so true—you can't beat a fresh herring!' To entertain themselves and to take their minds off the monotony of potatoes three times a day, family members would compete with one another for the most original way of expressing their fishy appreciation."

Thankfully, nowadays fish is easier to come by and we hope you enjoy this fishy favorite of ours. It's elegant enough for a party, but takes only a few minutes to prepare.

Halibut with Olive Sauce

4 4-ounce halibut filets

Olive oil

Salt and pepper

6 Kalamata olives, pitted

3 sun-dried tomatoes packed in oil, drained

¼ cup firmly packed fresh parsley leaves

3 tablespoons lemon juice

¼ cup olive oil

Prepare the barbecue grill or preheat the broiler. Brush the fish with a
touch of oil and sprinkle with salt and pepper. While the fish is cooking
(about 5 minutes per side), place the olives, tomatoes, parsley, and lemon
juice in a food processor and process until the mixture is finely chopped.
With the motor running, add the oil in a stream and blend until the sauce
is emulsified. Place in small bowl and allow each person to top their fish
with the sauce. Serves 4.

"Gastronomical perfection can be reached in these
combinations: one person dining alone, usually upon a couch
or a hillside; two persons, of no matter what sex or age, dining
in a good restaurant; six people, of no matter what
sex or age, dining in a good home."
—M.F.K. Fisher

My Kingdom for a Pizza

I t is impossible to say when pizza was invented, because it evolved over thousands of years, starting with the plain flat breads that go back as far as Neanderthal woman. The word itself, "whose mysterious roots might be Greco-Roman or Byzantine or Gothic-Longobard, was used as early as the year 997 at Gaeta, a port between Naples and Rome," according to *Treasures of the Italian Table* by Burton Anderson.

Regardless of its origins, pizza as we know it began to be developed in the eighteenth century when poor Neapolitans started putting tomatoes and garlic on top of bread and soon progressed to a wide variety of delicious toppings. But pizza was largely ignored by upper-crust Italians until 1889, when the beloved Queen Margherita, wife of King Umberto I, was asked to taste three kinds by pizzamaker Raffaele Esposito. She preferred the tomato-mozzarella-basil, which represented the *tricolore* flag of Italy. Rival pizzamakers complained this was not an original combination, but Esposito took credit for its creation nonetheless.

While pizza soon spread like wildfire in the U.S. (brought to New York in 1895 by immigrant Gennaro Lombardi), it was not until the last couple of decades that the pies truly caught on in Italy. Currently, Italians eat about forty-five pizzas per person per year, and the favorite continues to be the one named after the queen.

Pizza Margherita

Tomato Sauce

1 14½-ounce can tomato purée

Excellent!
May 98

1 clove garlic, crushed

½ teaspoon oregano

2 fresh basil leaves

Pepper to taste

No-Rise Pizza Dough

1 cup flour

Pinch salt

⅓ cup hot water

2 tablespoons olive oil

+ added
· artichoke hearts
· red pepper

1½ cups mozzarella cheese

8 black olives, pitted and sliced

6 large fresh basil leaves

To make the sauce, combine all the sauce ingredients in a medium saucepan. Cover and bring to a boil; then uncover and simmer, stirring occasionally, for 30 minutes.

Preheat the oven to 400 degrees. Mix the dough ingredients together and knead 5 minutes. Let rest 5 minutes. Roll out the dough on a cookie sheet; bake 5 to 7 minutes or until crispy. Remove from the oven and spread the sauce over it, leaving a ½-inch rim. Sprinkle the cheese over the sauce, then arrange the olives and basil decoratively. Bake 5 minutes. Makes 1 thin-crust pizza that serves 2 to 3.

Frida Kahlo

Probaby the most idolized woman artist of our time, **Frida Kahlo** suffered from a wide variety of horrific ailments in the course of her short life—many of which she depicted in her paintings. But this striking Mexican beauty never let her suffering get in the way of her joie de vivre. "What was Frida like?" asks biographer Raquel Tibol. "She was a tremendously powerful reactor who constantly spoke her mind . . . She decorated truth, invented it, shredded it, drew it out and provoked it, but she never misrepresented it."

Mesmerizing all who came into contact with her, including husband and fellow artist Diego Rivera and lover Leon Trotsky, "Frida was an enthusiast; she got the most out of everything," write her stepdaughter Guadalupe Rivera and Marie-Pierre Colle in *Frida's Fiestas*. "She celebrated saints' days, birthdays, baptisms, and most of the popular holidays, both religious and secular."

Celebrations meant food, including such taste treats as mole poblano and chicken escabeche, the preparation of which Frida oversaw. But her involvement went well beyond mere menu planning. "For Frida, setting the table was a ritual, whether she was unfolding the white openwork tablecloth from Aguascalientes, or arranging the simple plates that she customized with her initials, or setting out Spanish Talavera plates and handblown blue glasses and heirloom silverware. It was as if the shape and color and sound that was particular to each

individual object endowed it with life and an assigned place in a harmonious, aesthetically pleasing world."

Chicken Escabeche

6 boneless, skinless chicken breasts

1 cup white wine vinegar

2 medium onions, cut in half

3 carrots

1 celery stalk

1 bay leaf

1 sprig fresh thyme

1 sprig fresh oregano

Salt and pepper to taste

Sauce

2 onions, peeled and sliced

5 carrots, peeled and sliced

10 garlic cloves

½ to 1 cup olive oil

3 bay leaves

4 sprigs fresh oregano

3 sprigs fresh thyme

2 cups white wine vinegar

½ cup water

Combine the chicken breasts with the 1 cup vinegar, 2 medium onions, 3 carrots, celery stalk, bay leaf, thyme, oregano, salt, and pepper. Add water to cover, and cook until nearly tender.

While the chicken is cooking, make the sauce: Sauté the onions, carrots, and garlic in the oil until the onion is translucent. Add the herbs and sauté a minute longer. Add the vinegar and water and simmer for 10 minutes.

When the chicken is cooked through, remove from the cooking liquid and discard the liquid. Add the chicken to the sauce, bring to a boil, and simmer for 5 minutes. Remove from the heat and let the chicken in sauce cool completely, at least 2 hours in the refrigerator. Serve cold. Serves 8.

"Cooking tip: Wrap turkey leftovers in aluminum foil and throw them out."
—Nicole Hollander

Yes, She Has Some Bananas

Josephine Baker was only fifteen when she made her New York singing and dancing debut in 1921 in the all-black revue *Shuffle Along,* with songs by Eubie Blake and Noble Sissle; she did 504 performances before emigrating to Paris in 1925 to escape the racism of the United States. The epitome of a wild woman, Baker achieved instant fame as huge crowds rushed to see her nude stage show called La Revue Negre; to keep the momentum going, she also starred in the Folies Bergere wearing nothing but a G-string of bananas. By 1926, she had her own nightclub, impressing much of Paris—including visitor Ernest Hemingway—with her beauty and grace. Becoming a French citizen in 1937, she worked tirelessly for the French Army during World War II and later for the NAACP to help end racial prejudice in the United States. In her later years, she adopted twelve children of all races, dubbing them her "rainbow tribe."

During her heyday, one of her favorite luxuries was French champagne. She probably didn't frequent the kitchen herself, but she did ask chefs to incorporate champagne into her meals. We think she would have adored this dish.

Scallops in Champagne Sauce

(Nicole Alper)

2 tablespoons butter

1 teaspoon olive oil

20 scallops, seasoned with salt and pepper

1 cup champagne

½ cup fish stock

½ teaspoon grated lemon rind

½ teaspoon dried tarragon

¼ cup cream

1 cup champagne grapes

Fresh tarragon for garnish

In a large pan, melt 1 tablespoon of the butter with the oil and sear the seasoned scallops (about 30 seconds on each side). Remove from the pan and deglaze with the champagne. Add the fish stock, lemon rind, and tarragon, and reduce for several minutes over moderate heat. Add the cream and remaining butter, whisk until smooth, and adjust seasoning. Pour the sauce onto 4 individual plates and attractively arrange the scallops (per person) on top. Then scatter the champagne grapes over the scallops and garnish each plate with a sprig of tarragon. Serves 4.

Legend has it that the traditional wide, shallow-bowled wine glasses
were originally fashioned to the shape of
Marie Antoinette's breasts.

Of Women, Rice, and Chopsticks

Rice has a long association with women, according to Margaret Visser in *Much Depends on Dinner;* because of its lifegiving qualities, it is equated with a mother giving birth, while its whiteness is associated with female purity. These notions are supported by various Asian myths.

For example, "Thai villagers believe that the baby inside a pregnant woman sits in her stomach eating the food she eats. Because the woman eats mostly rice, the growing child body is thought to be made of rice. In the same way that women give their bodies to feed their children, so the Rice Mother goddess yields her body and soul to nourish the body of humankind," writes Jeremy MacClancy in *Consuming Culture.* "Thus villagers in Thailand, as well as parts of Burma, Malaysia, Bali, and Vietnam, see themselves as physically and psychically made up of rice."

Throughout Indonesia there is a myth that rice sprang from the body of a beautiful maiden. Her name was Samyam Sri and she was so stunning that the great god Batara Guru lusted after her and tried to rape her. The rest of the gods were horrified and decided that their only recourse to save Sri was to kill her (sound familiar?). "They buried her, lamenting dreadfully," writes Visser. "But in a very short time a miracle occurred: out of the body of the dead maiden grew rice (from her eyes), [and] sticky rice (from her chest). . . ."

While rice is ubiquitous throughout Asia, chopsticks are not. For reasons unbeknownst even to food historians, chopsticks are used in China, Japan, Vietnam, and Korea, but not in Thailand, Burma, Cambodia, and Laos. Chopsticks play an important role in the life of one of the most famous women in Japanese history, the Empress Jingu Kogo. Known as the Woman Warrior of

early Japan, she is said to have prepared for her fleet's successful invasion of Korea by spreading chopsticks over the ocean as an offering to the sea gods to ensure a safe and successful passage between the two lands. Because of her feats, the empress is revered even today by the Japanese navy as their patron saint. In honor of Jingu Kogo and the Rice Mother Goddess, we offer the following recipes. The first, being of Japanese origin, should be eaten with chopsticks. The second, inspired by Thailand, should not.

Tempura

½ cup konbu daishi (available at Japanese
markets, or substitute fish stock)

2 tablespoons soy sauce

2 tablespoons sake or rice wine

1 teaspoon sugar

1 egg

¾ cup cold water

1 cup unbleached flour

Batter. Excellent! Dec. 98

2 cups oil

1 sweet potato, peeled and cut into very thin slices

8 shiitake mushrooms, fresh or dried

8 green onions, cut into 3-inch lengths

2 green peppers, seeded and cut into quarters

12 jumbo shrimp, peeled and deveined

¼ cup grated daikon radish

1 teaspoon grated fresh ginger

In a saucepan, combine the konbu daishi or fish stock, soy sauce, sake, and sugar. Simmer for about 5 minutes and set aside.

In a medium bowl, beat the egg lightly. Add ¾ cup cold water and then the flour, stirring gently (some lumps are ok). Place the bowl containing the batter into an ice bath: cold batter results in crisp tempura.

In a wok, heat the oil to 350 degrees and make sure it stays at least this hot. Cook the tempura in batches, just a few pieces at a time, using two slotted spoons: one to put in the food and another one to take it out.

Dip each vegetable piece or shrimp in batter until lightly coated. Drop it into the oil and deep-fry until batter appears translucent. Remove and drain on paper towels.

Place the daikon and ginger in 4 small bowls. Pour the reserved sauce into each bowl and serve alongside the hot tempura. Serves 4.

Thai Chicken and Basil

Cooking Sauce

¾ cup canned coconut milk

3 tablespoons soy sauce

3 tablespoons rice vinegar

1½ tablespoons fish sauce or soy sauce

½ to 1 teaspoon crushed dried hot red chilies

—————

White rice

6 dried shiitake mushrooms

2 tablespoons vegetable oil

1 medium-size onion, thinly sliced

3 cloves garlic, pressed or minced

2 tablespoons minced fresh ginger

2 pounds boneless skinless chicken breasts,
cut crosswise into ¼-inch-wide strips

1½ cups lightly packed slivered fresh basil leaves

Combine the ingredients for the cooking sauce in a small bowl. Prepare the rice according to the package directions.

Woman's Country

Kogo was not the only powerful Japanese empress. The earliest known Chinese references to Japan refer to it as "Queen's Country." Indeed, many if not most of the legendary leaders of Japan prior to the arrival of the Chinese were women. Many historians claim that in its earliest history, Japan was a society dominated by women. By the seventh century, however, it was back to the kitchen—even though the last of the women empresses were still on the throne, they had become mere figureheads.

In a bowl, soak the mushrooms in hot water to cover until soft, 10 to 15 minutes. Lift the mushrooms from the water, squeeze dry, and trim off and discard the tough stems. Cut the caps into ¼-inch slivers and set aside.

In a 10- to 12-inch frying pan or a wok over high heat, heat 1 tablespoon oil. Add the onion, garlic, and ginger; stir-fry until the onion is a light gold color. Scoop the vegetables into a bowl and set aside.

Add the chicken strips to the pan, one third at a time; stir occasionally until the meat is tinged with brown, about 3 minutes. Lift the strips from the pan and reserve with the cooked vegetables. Repeat to cook the remaining chicken; add oil if needed to prevent sticking.

Pour the cooking sauce into the pan and boil until reduced by one third. Return the onion and chicken to the pan. Add the basil and mushrooms; stir to heat through. Serve over rice. Serves 4.

"What I love about cooking is that after a hard day, there is something comforting about the fact that if you melt butter and add flour, then hot stock, it will get thick! It's a sure thing. It's a sure thing in a world where nothing is sure!"
—Nora Ephron

Sizzling Snacks and Sandwiches

Breaking Bread with Golda

in 1969, **Golda Meir**, a Russian-born, Milwaukee-raised Jew, was sworn in as Israel's fourth premier and governed for five embattled years. Foreign minister from 1956 to 1966 and before that the minister of labor, she was opposed by Agudat Israel, an Orthodox religious party whose members believed that Jewish men should not look at "strange women." Despite this, Golda had no use for "women's liberation," claiming that "It's the men who are discriminated against. They can't bear children. And no one's likely to do anything about it."

Until she resigned a month into her second term, citing schisms in her party due to military planning mistakes, Meir was a decision-maker who was eager to hear the opinions of others.

"The unlikely place where this deliberative process took place," writes Robert Slater, in *Golda, The Uncrowned Queen of Israel,* "was Golda's kitchen.

There her permanent entourage of Labor Party advisers gathered, usually on Saturday evenings, to prepare for the regular Sunday cabinet meeting. The kitchen meetings led cynics to remark that decisions which rightly belonged to the whole cabinet had been 'baked' in advance. . . .

"The 'Kitchen Cabinet' meetings were far more frank than those of the full cabinet. There were no stenographers, formal votes, or leaks to the press. The charge that the Kitchen Cabinet was fundamentally undemocratic mattered little

to Golda. She ruled her government with an iron hand, and it fazed her not at all that major decisions were made around her green formica kitchen table the night before the issues at hand would be brought up for consideration by the formal cabinet. At home or in her office Golda was the boss."

Golda did at least a little genuine cooking in her kitchen, if not on Saturday nights. She was famous, at least in the eyes of her grandson, Gideon, for her gefilte fish. But as she herself admitted with a laugh, Gideon was hardly unprejudiced.

Golda, in her lengthy tableside political talks, undoubtedly broke bread with many important foreign dignitaries. Here is a recipe for challah—the Jewish braided bread eaten on the Sabbath. It's great any time of the week.

Challah

1 package dry yeast

½ cup warm water

4 cups all-purpose flour

2 tablespoons vegetable oil

2 teaspoons salt

2 tablespoons sugar (or less to taste)

2 eggs, beaten

1 egg yolk

1 teaspoon cold water

Preheat the oven to 350 degrees. Dissolve the yeast in the warm water. Set aside. In large mixing bowl, pour in flour and make a well in the center;

set aside. In large mixing bowl pour in the hot water, followed by the oil, salt, and sugar. When the sugar has dissolved, and the liquid mixture has cooled to a lukewarm temperature, add the yeast. Then add the two beaten eggs. Mix well. Add the flour to the yeast mixture, half a cup at a time.

Turn onto a floured surface and knead well. Place dough in a greased bowl, cover with a clean cloth, and let rise for two hours, until it about doubles in size. Knead again, then divide the dough into three equal parts. Pinch one end of all three pieces together and then braid. Pinch the other ends together when done braiding. Place on greased and floured baking pan. Let rise 25 minutes. Combine the egg yolk and 1 teaspoon cold water. Brush over the braided dough. Bake for 10 to 15 minutes at 400 degrees and then lower temperature to 350 degrees and continue baking for an additional 45 minutes. Makes 1 challah.

"I like the philosophy of the sandwich, as it were. It typifies my attitude to life, really. It's all there, it's fun, it looks good, and you don't have to wash up afterwards."
—Molly Parkin

Tea Anyone?

We have Anna, the seventh **Duchess of Bedford**, to thank for the custom of afternoon tea. Among the aristocrats of her generation (the late 1700s), it was customary to down a huge breakfast, nibble at lunch, and consume a substantial dinner—but not until at least 8 P.M. On such a diet, Anna would get what she described as "a sinking feeling" by five in the afternoon. To allay this discomfort, she would order tea and cakes served, and promptly started a fashion amongst all her starving cohorts. "Snacking on sandwiches and pastries followed by tea became a habit among the aristocracy," reports James Norwood in *Tea Lover's Treasury*, "and soon developed into a ritual—usually the pleasantest ritual of the day. As it began, so it remained essentially a female ritual."

Such a "ladies' event" was brought to full perfection by Queen Mary in the early twentieth century. "Everything had to be fully ready by 4 P.M. punctually," writes Charles Oliver in *Dinner at Buckingham Palace,* "with sandwiches, cakes and biscuits invitingly set out on gleaming silver dishes upon a smoothly-running trolley. The teapot, cream jug, hot-water jug and sugar bowl were always the same antique silver service which had been a favorite of Queen Victoria ... [Later] Queen Mary would take over and meticulously measure out her favorite Indian tea (Queen Mary Tea Twinings; a fine Darjeeling with a pronounced muscatel flavor) from a jade tea-caddy she kept locked in a cupboard. Then she would pour on the boiling water and complete the tea-making ritual by snuffing out the spirit stove before sitting back for the footmen to pour tea and hand round sandwiches and cakes. But before Queen Mary gave the signal for this to begin she would always let exactly three minutes elapse from the moment she poured hot water on the tea leaves so that the tea would be perfectly brewed."

If you want to try this "female ritual" on your own, we offer one traditional item often seen at such events—scones—and two more modern items.

Golden Raisin Scones

Good! May 98

2 cups all-purpose flour

1 tablespoon baking powder

3 tablespoons sugar

½ teaspoon salt

½ teaspoon ground nutmeg

1 stick butter, cut into cubes

1 extra large egg

⅓ cup cream

¾ cup golden raisins

Combine the dry ingredients in a large bowl. Add the cold butter and combine with your fingers until the mixture resembles coarse meal.

Break the egg into a small bowl and whisk lightly. Combine half the beaten egg and ½ cup of the cream and pour this liquid over the flour mixture and combine until well mixed. (Add more cream a drop at a time if too dry.) Scrape the dough onto a lightly floured work surface.

Gently knead in the raisins. Roll the dough to ½ inch thick and cut into 2¼-inch rounds with a biscuit cutter. Place on ungreased baking sheet and chill for 15 minutes.

Preheat the oven to 450 degrees. Add the 1 tablespoon milk to the remaining egg and brush the top of each scone with the egg mixture. Bake until the tops are lightly colored, about 15 minutes. Cool on wire racks for 10 minutes and serve warm. Makes 12.

Mango Chutney and Smoked Turkey Triangles

(Lynette Rohrer)

9x13-inch piece of focaccia bread

4 ounces goat cheese

4 ounces cream cheese

½ cup mango chutney

8 ounces smoked turkey slices

1 cup arugula

Carefully slice the focaccia in half horizontally, to create a top and bottom. Combine the goat and cream cheese and spread it on the bottom half. Spread a layer of chutney. Lay the turkey and arugula on top, cover with the top half of the focaccia and cut into 1″ x 3″ fingers. Makes 3 dozen.

———————

"Ah, there's nothing like tea in the afternoon. When the British Empire collapses, historians will find that it had made but two invaluable contributions to civilization—this tea ritual and the detective novel."

—Ayn Rand

Salmon Pinwheels

1 large unsliced sandwich loaf

¼ cup butter, softened

2 ounces watercress

¼ pound thinly sliced smoked salmon

Salt and pepper to taste

1 teaspoon lemon juice

Remove the crust from the bread and cut two 2-inch-thick slices lengthwise. Roll flat with a rolling pin. Spread butter over slices. Layer the watercress leaves and then layer the salmon on top. Season with salt and pepper and sprinkle with lemon juice. Roll up each from the short end and wrap in plastic wrap. Refrigerate. When ready to serve remove the plastic and slice into 7 pinwheels per roll. Makes 14.

She Should Have Been A "Tea-totaler"

In 1751, finding her married lover unacceptable to her father, Mary Blandy persuaded the lover to supply her with a love philter to change her parent's mind. He provided her with arsenic, of which she was aware—as a letter she wrote later proved—and she used it in her father's tea. Papa died and Mary was found guilty of murder. "Gentlemen," she said on the scaffold, "do not hang me high, for the sake of decency."

The Picky Princess of Pepperidge

Margaret Fogarty Rudkin made her first loaf of whole wheat bread in 1937 at the age of forty, when she set up an oven in her stockbroker husband's polo pony stable in rural Connecticut. Thus began a home business that started with sales to neighbors and eventually became the multimillion-dollar Pepperidge Farms, named after a pepperidge tree in the enterprising baker's front yard. She sold her bread with little advertising because of a commitment to high quality, whatever the cost: the flour used was unbleached and stone-ground; the bread was cut and kneaded by hand; and only sweet butter was allowed—no commercial shortenings were permitted to touch her loaves. By 1940, she had outgrown the stables and expanded her baking facilities to a plant in Norwalk, Connecticut, where she branched out into cookies and other baked goods. These days, Pepperidge Farms is owned by some corporate megagiant and if you want the kind of bread that would make Margie proud, you'll have to bake it yourself.

Whole Wheat Bread

For the yeast:

1 cup milk

1 cup water

1 tablespoon shortening or lard

1 tablespoon butter

2 tablespoons sugar

1 tablespoon salt

¼ cup warm water (105 to 115 degrees)

1 package active dry yeast

For the bread:

1 beaten egg

¼ cup melted butter

2½ cups lukewarm water

1½ teaspoons salt

¼ to ½ cup sugar, honey, or maple syrup

4 cups whole-grain flour

4 cups all-purpose flour

Scald the milk and add 1 cup water, the shortening or lard, butter, sugar, and salt. In a separate large bowl, combine the warm water and yeast. Let dissolve 3 to 5 minutes. If using compressed yeast, crumble 1 cake yeast into ¼ cup 85-degree water and let stand 8 to 10 minutes. Add the luke-warm milk mixture to the dissolved yeast.

Beat together the egg, melted butter, lukewarm water, salt, and sugar, honey, or maple syrup. Add this mixture to the yeast mixture. Add, without sifting, a mixture of whole-grain flour and the all-purpose flour. Mix in half the required flour gradually and beat about 1 minute. Then, as the rest of the flour is added, lay aside the spoon and mix by hand. When the dough begins to leave the sides of the bowl, turn it out onto a lightly floured board or pastry cloth. (To flour a board lightly and evenly, allow

about 1 tablespoon flour for each cup of flour in the recipe.) A damp towel placed under the board will keep it from slipping. Turn the dough several times to make it easier to handle. Cover the dough with a cloth and let it rest for 10 to 15 minutes before kneading.

Knead the dough until it becomes smooth and elastic, then place it in a large greased bowl. Turn the dough over until the entire surface of the dough is lightly greased. Cover the bowl with a cloth and set the dough to rise until it doubles in bulk, usually 1 to 2 hours. To test if the dough has risen sufficiently, poke it with your fingertips. If the imprint of your fingertips remains in the dough, it has risen enough. (Note: At high altitudes yeast bread dough rises more rapidly and may become overproofed if not watched carefully and allowed to rise only until doubled in bulk.)

Now punch down the dough with a balled hand. Work the edges to the center and turn the bottom to the top. Divide it into three equal pieces and shape them lightly into mounds; place them on a floured board, cover with a cloth, and allow them to rest 10 minutes. Form each into a loaf by using a rolling pin or your palm to flatten it into an oblong first, then roll it into a loaf. Compress the short ends with your hands and seal the loaf, folding under any excess as you slide the dough, seam side down, into the greased pan. The finished ends of the loaf should fit against the short

"Bread that must be sliced with an ax is
bread that is too nourishing."
—Fran Lebowitz

ends of the pan to help support the dough as it rises. When the loaf is in the pan, you may grease its top lightly.

Cover the pan with a cloth and let rise. The dough will eventually fill out to the corners of the pan. While it is rising—to almost, but not quite, double in bulk—preheat the oven to 350 degrees. When ready to bake, the loaf will be symmetrical and a slight impression will remain when you press lightly with your finger. Bake for about 45 minutes. When done, the loaf will shrink away slightly from the sides of the pan. You can test for doneness by tapping the bottom of the pan to release the loaf, then tapping the bottom of the loaf. If it makes a hollow sound, the bread is done. Makes 3 loaves.

We're the Second Banana, Even in Bread

According to food historian Reay Tannahill, the word "lord" is derived from the Old English *hlaford,* meaning "keeper of the bread" or loaf—that is, master of the household. "Lady" comes from *hlaefdigge,* meaning "kneader of the dough" or "second-most-important person."

Cake, Brioche, What's the Diff?

So maybe **Marie Antoinette**, wife of Louis XVI, didn't say "let them eat cake" when informed that the French people had no bread to eat. It was written up by Jean-Jacque Rousseau in his 1769 *Confessions* where he claimed the remark was made by "a great princess." At the time Marie was but an eleven-year-old autocrat-in-training in Austria, and didn't become queen of France for five more years. But it made good copy years later when revolutionaries were looking for inflammatory slogans. Others insist she did make a similar remark, but was misquoted; what she really said was, "Let them eat brioche," a kind of yeast bun.

As an adult, she could have easily said similar things, displaying a flagrant disregard for everything but her own pleasure and openly plotting intrigues against other well-to-do ladies such as the Comtesse de La Motte and Madame du Barry. These licentious ladies had too much time on their hands.

Regardless of what she said, however, it was food that led to her ultimate demise. Fleeing from the revolutionaries, the royal family was caught in June 1791 just one hundred miles outside Paris, where they had stopped to dine. Before her beheading two years later, however, Marie was one well-fed jailbird. According to Benjamin Franklin, while she was in prison, a staff of thirteen prepared dinners and suppers for her, consisting of "three soups, four entrées, three roast dishes, each of three pieces, four sweet courses, a plate of fancy cakes, three compotes, three

dishes of fruit, three loaves of bread with butter, one bottle of Champagne, one small carafe of Bordeaux, one of Malvoisie, one of Madeira and four cups of coffee." History doesn't record how hefty the former royal was when she met the guillotine.

Even though we don't believe for a minute that Marie recommended brioche to the commoners of France, we thought we'd take the opportunity to present them to you. Ours, made without yeast, is inspired by Alice B. Toklas, a Parisian resident for many years who managed to keep her head.

Brioche

1 tablespoon water

3 teaspoons baking powder

4 tablespoons milk (can be lowfat)

1 cup sugar

1 tablespoon rum (or substitute water)

2 cups all-purpose flour

4 eggs

¾ cup softened butter

————   ————

"What is sauce for the goose may be sauce for the gander
but it is not necessarily sauce for the chicken,
the turkey, or the guinea hen."
—Alice B. Toklas

In a small bowl, combine the water and baking powder. Add the milk, sugar, and rum. Stir well and set aside.

Sift flour into a large bowl. Add the eggs and combine until completely smooth. Add the sugar mixture and mix thoroughly. Add the butter, mix well, and set aside in a cool place (not in the refrigerator) for 12 hours. Pour into a deep round buttered brioche mold and bake for about 30 minutes in 375-degree oven. Makes 1 brioche.

Boy Do You Look Nice Tonight!

In 1786, an ingenious entrepreneur, Antoine-Auguste Parmentier, persuaded Louis XVI to encourage the cultivation of potatoes by lending him one hundred useless acres outside of Paris. Then, to promote the eating of potatoes, Parmentier convinced the king to hold a banquet and serve only potato dishes. He even talked Marie Antoinette into wearing potato flowers in her hair.

It must not have been one of her best nights—have you ever seen potato flowers? Tiny, believe us, they are nothing to crow about. In any case, Parmentier's plot worked and the tubers caught on like, well, hot potatoes.

One More Antoinette Tale

During the Turkish siege of Vienna in 1638, bakers were at work one night in underground bakehouses making bread for the next day when they heard a rhythmic thumping. Guessing that the Turks were driving a mine, two of them alerted the commandant of Vienna and, getting directions from the sound, the Austrians dug a second tunnel and exploded a powerful countermine.

As a reward for their intelligence, the baker boys were granted the privilege of creating a rich roll in the shape of a crescent, the Turkish emblem. These rolls became enormously popular with the Viennese, who called them *kipferl*. When Marie Antoinette left Vienna to marry Louis XVI, she missed these tasty treats so much that she sent for an Austrian baker to teach his Paris confrères how to make them. Transplanted as croissants, they became yet another "French" delicacy introduced by a foreign queen.

Anyone who has been to Paris knows of the joys of walking along the narrow streets at dawn, with the delicious aroma of freshly baking croissants wafting all around you. "The closest thing to Paris I've ever found," writes Nicole, "is the Delanghe Patisserie on the corner of Filmore and Bush streets in San Francisco. I used to see them, a husband and wife team, busily rolling, folding, and baking in the wee hours of the morn. Their product speaks for itself—croissants drenched in real butter, made the old-fashioned way. With bakeries like this in existence, it seems counter intuitive to attempt the process at home, but I can assure you, nothing beats the smell and taste of a genuinely homemade croissant."

Pastisserie Delanghe's Croissants

1½ tablespoons salt

6 tablespoons sugar

2 ounces yeast

2 cups milk

2 pounds all-purpose flour

¼ pound butter

All the ingredients should be at room temperature before you start, except the butter, which should be cold but not hard. Dissolve the salt, sugar, and yeast in the milk. In a large bowl, add the flour and pour in the milk mixture. Mix well and then knead for 5 minutes. Cover and let rest for 45 minutes in the refrigerator.

Dust a board with flour and roll the dough into a 12x8-inch rectangle. Cut butter into small pieces and lay them over half the dough and then fold the other half over. Roll into an 18x6-inch rectangle and let rest for 30 minutes in the refrigerator. Repeat the folding process 2 more times with a 30-minute rest in between rolls.

Roll the dough into a narrow strip and cut the strip in half lengthwise. Cut triangles into each strip. Roll the triangular pieces beginning with the widest edge, stretching them slightly as you roll. Shape the rolls into crescents.

Preheat oven to 400 degrees. Place crescents on greased baking sheet. Bake for 10 minutes and reduce heat to 350 degrees and bake until done, about 10 to 15 minutes longer. Makes 30 croissants.

Somebody Must Be Making Those Things

If there were an award given to the woman in the kitchen the world most likes to dish, Martha Stewart would win hands down. Her *Martha Stewart Living* was parodied as *Is Martha Stewart Living?*, catty articles regularly appear in national magazines about her choice in houses and mates, and she has been dubbed the "hostess from hell" by the *Boston Globe*. Stories abound about her workaholic perfectionism—lambasting assistants for substituting a glass bowl with a thin blue stripe instead of a clear glass bowl because "food doesn't look as good in stripes." In the food world, there seems to be some resistance to accepting her as a bona fide cook, despite her many cookbooks. *The Food Chronology*, an encyclopedia of food facts, calls her a "U.S. promoter" rather than a chef and goes on to say that her 1982 cookbook *Entertaining* "contains recipes that are mostly either derivative, overdifficult, or just plain don't work, but seductive illustrations (deep-dish pies inside woven baskets, poached pears with candied violets in a crystal bowl filled with wine, and the like) began a multi-million dollar empire of magazines, books, and videotapes."

As we go to press, her latest cookbook is on national bestseller lists and she currently nets over two million dollars a year. She didn't coin the phrase, "Living well is the best revenge"—but she might as well have.

Naughty Natalie

atalie Barney was a beautiful, rich American teenager when she first went to Paris in the early 1900s and fell in love with the leading courtesan of the day, a woman named Liane de Pougy. When her father heard of the affair, he caught the first boat and carried her back to America in disgrace. But before he could marry Natalie off and keep her from "female temptations," he died, leaving her his entire fortune.

Too bad, Dad. Natalie returned to Paris at the age of twenty-one and proceeded to establish a salon at 20 Rue Jacob where, for the next sixty years, she entertained most of the noteworthy French, British, and American authors at her Friday evenings. Natalie penned a few slight volumes of her own, including *Pénsées d'une Amazone (Thoughts of an Amazon)*, but was much more well-known for the works she inspired. She was celebrated in Djuna Barnes' *Ladies Almanack* and Radclyffe Hall's *The Well of Loneliness*—the most renowned lesbian novel of the day—to name but two.

At her salons, Natalie was known for her cucumber sandwiches, a food item that has gone out of favor in recent decades. Perhaps in honor of this truly wild woman, we can bring them back into fashion. It's best to make these just before serving, since they tend to get soggy if they sit around.

Cucumber and Dill Heart Sandwiches

½ medium-sized cucumber, peeled and sliced very thin

Salt

2 tablespoons butter, softened

8 slices white bread

2 tablespoons oil

1 teaspoon lemon juice

1 teaspoon vinegar

1 teaspoon chopped fresh dill

Lightly salt the cucumber slices and place them in a colander for about 20 minutes. Pat dry. Spread the butter on the bread. Combine the cucumbers, oil, lemon juice, vinegar, and dill. Make attractive layers of the cucumber on 4 slices of the bread. Cover with the remaining bread and cut out hearts with a heart-shaped cookie cutter (or any shape you like). Makes 16 sandwiches.

———————— 🍴 ————————

"It was the usual 'zoo tea.' You know, we eat—the others watch."
—Princess Margaret of England, on public receptions attended
by royalty in 1954

A Heart of Gold

Pocahontas has become quite famous of late, although in reality she looked nothing like the Disney glamour girl who recently graced the silver screen. But she does deserve recognition by at least some Americans—ten million people now trace their ancestry to the folks she saved.

In case you missed it, here's how the story goes. Only 38 of the 105 members of the Jamestown colony in Virginia lived out its first winter, and all of them probably would have perished had not Pocahontas intervened to save the life of Captain John Smith, or so the story goes. In 1608, Smith was captured by the Powhatan chief Wahunsonacook, who was about to kill him when, according to Smith's account (written in the third person and published in 1624, its veracity is questioned by certain historians) "Pocahontas, the king's dearest daughter . . . got his head in her arms and laid her own upon his to save him from death." Later the Powhatan powerhouse bartered for maize to feed Smith and his famished compatriots, which was the only reason they didn't die of starvation.

As whites of the time were wont to do, they didn't return the favor. In 1613, the very same colonists kidnapped Pocahontas and held her for ransom; when the money from her father was not forthcoming, she was instructed in Christianity and baptized as Rebecca. The next year, when she was about eighteen years old, she married widower John Rolfe, the main force in persuading the

Virginia colonists to grow tobacco. A few years later, the happy couple went to England for a visit where she was presented at the court of James I and was disgruntled to run into John Smith. Just before the return voyage, Pocahontas caught a virus and died at about the age of twenty-one.

Confetti Corn Bread

1 cup cornmeal

1 cup all-purpose flour

¼ cup sugar

1 tablespoon baking powder

1 teaspoon salt

⅓ cup oil

1 egg

1 cup milk

¼ cup diced roasted red peppers

1 teaspoon finely crumbled rosemary

Preheat the oven to 400 degrees. Combine the dry ingredients in a bowl and mix well. In a separate bowl, combine the oil, egg, and milk. Mix well. Stir the liquids into the dry ingredients until just blended. Add the peppers and rosemary and stir. Pour the batter into a well-buttered 8-inch-square pan. Bake for 25 minutes or until done. Serves 6.

Taming the Wild Blueberry

lizabeth White is given credit for provoking the cultivation of the blueberry by offering prizes in the late 1800s for the largest wild blueberry. The Department of Agriculture got wind of her project and started crossbreeding the winners in 1909. The rest, as they say, is blueberry history. Where Liz lived (Maine, we would guess, since it is blueberry country), why she gave blueberry prizes, and other seemingly pertinent facts have been lost in the annals of time. Even *The Food Chronology* tells us nothing. But don't despair, this Blueberry Blintz recipe is so good you won't care how the blueberries got there. They are often served at breakfast, but make a tasty snack or dessert.

Blueberry Blintzes

1 cup all-purpose flour

½ teaspoon salt

4 eggs

1 cup water or milk

Butter

2 cups blueberries, well washed

2 tablespoons sugar

2 tablespoons all-purpose flour

Applesauce

Sour cream

In a medium bowl, sift together the flour and salt. In a large bowl, beat the eggs, add the water, and beat again. Gradually add the salted flour to the eggs, stirring constantly to make a thin, smooth batter.

Lightly grease a 6-inch skillet with butter and place over a moderately high flame. Pour about ½ cup of the batter into the skillet. Fry until the blintz begins to "blister" and the edges curl away from the skillet; the top of the blintz may be slightly moist. Turn out, fried side up, by inverting the skillet over a wooden board. It may be necessary to tap the edge of the skillet against the board. [Note: The skillet should be greased about every third blintz.]

When the blintzes are all fried, sprinkle the blueberries with sugar and flour. Place 1 tablespoon blueberries in the center of each blintz (browned side up). Fold over one side of the dough to cover the filling, then overlap with the other side of the dough. Tuck both sides under so that they almost meet at the back center. Again fry in butter until lightly browned on both sides. Serve hot with applesauce or sour cream. Serves 6.

"I had left home (like all Jewish girls) in order to eat pork
and take birth control pills. When I first shared an intimate evening
with my husband I was swept away by the passion (so dormant inside
myself) of a long and tortured existence. The physical cravings
I had tried so hard to deny finally and ultimately sated...
but enough about the pork."
—Roseanne

Savory and Unsavory Tarts

Goddess of the Kitchen

Novelist Barbara Quick had the pleasure of knowing M.F. K. Fisher in her later years and has this to say:

Although **Mary Frances Kennedy Fisher** (1908–1992) was one of our preeminent writers on food and the art of eating, she is remembered as much more than a food writer. W.H. Auden once said of her, "I do not know anyone in the United States who writes better prose." The author of over twenty books on food, life, and travel, M.F.K. Fisher has what amounts to a cult following. She was one of the first Californians to "discover" French food, and is credited by Alice Waters and others as being the godmother of the much-touted California cuisine.

Married three times (always with the best intentions), Mary Frances created an aura of romance and artistry wherever she lived, whether in Dijon of the 1920s, Depression-era Laguna Beach, or among the terraced vineyards of a medieval village in Switzerland overlooking Lac Léman. Quoted in a *Time* magazine profile, she once said, "We have to eat to live, and we might as well do it with fun and panache and style."

As an old woman Mary Frances lived in Last House, a custom-designed, one-person home built for her by her friend and patron David Bouverie, nestled in the meadows of Bouverie's five-hundred-acre Sonoma County, California ranch. Friends and fans would leave daily offerings of fruit, vegetables, and flowers on her doorstep, as if at the altar of a rural goddess. Ironically, the doyenne of cuisine was all too rarely invited out to dinner—people often felt too intimidated to cook for the witty and sometimes sharp-tongued Mary Frances. She told me how she once, in her younger years, invited a tableful of St. Helena neighbors over and served a dinner consisting entirely of canned food, just to see if anyone would have the nerve to comment or complain. No one did.

When guests would come to stay at Last House, Mary Frances, too infirm by then to do the cooking herself, would direct them in the preparation of food from her wheelchair, waving her hands in the air like a geriatric Titiana. "I love being old," she said. "It's considered perfectly all right to just sit here and order everyone else about."

Every evening Mary Frances would leave her wheelchair to walk with the tentativeness of a large egret or a heron (she was 5'8" in her unbent days) to the thronelike wicker chair on her west-facing porch. She was faithful to the ritual of watching the sunset, sipping her favorite mixture of white wine and Campari. "An innocent sky," she murmured one evening, half to herself, when the sunset colors gave way to darkness.

"Innocent" is also the word she used to describe the bread pudding she liked to serve to her guests at Last House before they retired for the night to the sleeping porch with its sounds of crickets or rain.

Bread Pudding
(As dictated by M.F.K. Fisher to Barbara Quick)

4 slices dry French bread

Sweet butter

½ cup raisins

1 cup water or wine or booze, approximately

2 eggs

1 pint milk

1 teaspoon pure vanilla extract or rum

½ cup brown sugar

Nutmeg

Cream

A Feast for the Eyes

Five of M.F.K. Fisher's memorable volumes have been collected together in *The Art of Eating,* which, if you enjoy fine writing by feisty females, is not to be missed. Her unique approach to food writing can't really be described, only experienced. So here's a short excerpt from *An Alphabet of Gourmets,* written in 1949, to whet your appetite. Enjoy!

"B is for Bachelors . . . and the wonderful dinners they pull out of their cupboards with such dining-room aplomb and kitchen chaos.

"Their approach to gastronomy is basically sexual, since few of them under seventy-nine will bother to produce a good meal unless it is for a pretty woman. Few of them at any age will consciously ponder on the aphrodisiac qualities of the dishes they serve forth, but subconsciously they use what tricks they have to make their little banquets, whether intimate or merely convivial, lead as subtly as possible to the hoped-for bedding down."

Thickly butter 4 slices of dry French bread (it should be sweet butter and bread that has some substance—no limp white bread for this). Cut it into bite-size pieces.

Plump a half a cup of raisins in water or wine or booze. Beat two eggs in a pint of milk. Add some vanilla or rum, and ½ cup brown sugar.

Put half of the bread nibbles in the top of a double boiler. Add half the raisins and half the liquid. Then add the rest of the bread, raisins, and liquid. Put some nutmeg on top.

Cover closely. Put over generously boiling water. Turn down the heat. Don't peek for 70 minutes. Then take the lid off, let the pudding cool, and turn it out onto a pudding dish. Serve with cream. Serves 4.

"Sharing food with another human being is an intimate act
that should not be indulged in lightly."
—M.F.K. Fisher

A Sensible Meal

With the making of Ang Lee's *Sense and Sensibility,* starring Emma Thompson; the television dramatization of *Pride and Prejudice*; and the movie *Persuasion,* the world is experiencing a rekindling of its love affair with **Jane Austen**, the nineteenth-century English author who wrote on the timeless issues of class and romance. Often regarded as the greatest woman writer of all time, Austen passed her days, as did most English ladies of the period, almost exclusively with her own family. She didn't involve herself in literary circles, but rather occupied herself when not writing by playing with her nieces and nephews. Never married, she did have a brief attachment to a clergyman who died before they could become engaged. From this sheltered life, however, she created the stuff of great art; her novels are noted for their satirical wit and complex view of human nature.

While such a life could scarcely be considered "wild," her unfailing awareness of the constrictions placed on women by social conventions has helped many a woman break free from such constraints. Indeed, her entire oeuvre can be seen as a meditation on the narrow range of options presented to nineteenth -century women, and her popularity today speaks to the continued struggle with these issues that women feel.

As part of the Jane Austen revival, two women, Maggie Black and Deirdre LeFaye, recently compiled a book of recipes, many of which were written by people closely connected to the English novelist. Though not all the recipes can be immediately traced to her active quill, they are foods that she and her characters (had they been real) would have eaten at the time. One such item is Lemon Mincemeat, a modern version of which is given here.

Lemon Mincemeat

1 large lemon

2½ cups currants

1 cup hard green apple, chopped

1¼ cups white sugar

⅔ cup cut mixed lemon peel

1½ cups shredded beef suet

½ teaspoon grated nutmeg

½ teaspoon ground cinnamon

¼ teaspoon ground mace

¼ teaspoon salt

Pinch of freshly ground black pepper

1 tablespoon orange-flower water

5 tablespoons Malaga wine or brandy

Squeeze the lemon and strain the juice. Set the juice aside. Boil the pulp and rind in a small saucepan until soft, then process to a paste in an electric blender.

Prehat the oven to 250 degrees. In a large ovenproof pan, add all the dry ingredients, mix thoroughly, then add the lemon paste and all the liquids, including the lemon juice. Stir well. Cook in the oven for 1 hour. May be stored in the refrigerator in glass jars for later use to fill pie crusts.

Bubble, Bubble, Toil and Trouble

María Prophetíssima, a resident of Alexandria in the first century A.D., goes down in history as the inventor of a kitchen item still in use today—the double boiler. It was an accident; as Vicki León tells us in *Uppity Women of Ancient Times,* "María's real love affair was with alchemy, not haute cuisine." Alchemy was the forerunner of modern chemistry, a mystical quest to "find the essence of that which is bodily, and embody that which is spirit" which consisted of combining various substances over heat to discover the Philosopher's Stone, a primal material that would turn everything it touched into gold.

In her quest, María did come up with the first still; however "there's no evidence that this three-part apparatus helped her find the Philosopher's Stone," explains León, "but it came in mighty handy for distilling perfume and other substances. María then came up with the *kerotakis,* a covered pot whose vapors could waft over gold leaf and other esoteric (and expensive) ingredients to produce the desired effect. No show on the Stone again, but now María had a double boiler, useful for making a nice egg custard to keep her spirits up after these dead ends."

The zesty Alexandrian never did figure out how to turn lead into gold, but she did publish a "cookbook" of her alchemical recipes and her memory lives on today—cooks in France and Spain still call their double boiler *"le bain de Marie"* or *"baño-María,"* which translates as Mary's bath. Here the double boiler is used for three sinfully rich chocolate desserts.

Chocolate Fondue with Strawberries

(Nicole Alper)

6 ounces semisweet chocolate

⅓ cup heavy cream

2 tablespoons Grand Marnier

2 baskets fresh whole strawberries

Melt the chocolate over a *bain marie*. Whisk in the cream. Add the Grand Marnier to taste. Pour into a fondue dish. Serve with the berries for dipping. For a colorful and romantic touch, sprinkle a silver platter with wild flowers, put the fondue dish in the center, and scatter the berries around it. Serves 4.

Banana-Almond Chocolate Mousse

(Nicole Alper)

8 ounces semisweet chocolate

3 ounces butter, softened

3 eggs, separated

1 cup almonds

"Research tells us that fourteen out of any ten individuals like chocolate."

—Sandra Boynton

2 large bananas, slightly ripe
(reserve a few slices for garnish)

---

1 cup heavy cream, placed in an ice bath

¼ cup fine granulated sugar

1 tablespoon powdered sugar

1 sprig of fresh mint

In a stainless steel bowl melt the chocolate over a *bain marie*. Once the chocolate is completely melted, whisk in the butter, a bit at a time. Add the egg yolks to the mixture, one by one.

Grind the almonds in a food processor, add the bananas, and process until smooth; add to the chocolate mixture. Now whisk the egg whites, adding the granulated sugar a spoonful at a time, until they form soft white peaks. Pour the chocolate-banana mixture down the side of the bowl containing the egg whites, and gently fold until they are combined. Now beat the cream over the ice bath until it begins to thicken. Once the cream forms ripples on the surface when it falls from the whisk, it is ready to be gently folded into the egg whites.

Pour the mousse into a decorative ramekin and chill for at least 1 hour. Before serving, garnish with banana slices, powdered sugar, and a sprig of mint. Serves 6 to 8.

Mexican Hot Chocolate

2 ounces unsweetened chocolate

2 cups milk (can be low- or nonfat)

1 cup heavy cream (can substitute half-and-half)

6 tablespoons sugar

½ to 1 teaspoon ground cinnamon

1 teaspoon pure vanilla extract

In the top of a *bain marie,* melt the chocolate. In a separate pot over medium-low heat, heat the milk and cream until hot but not boiling. Be careful not to scorch. When the milk is hot, add a bit to the melted chocolate and mix well. Then stir in the rest of the milk, and add the sugar, cinnamon, and vanilla. With the *bain marie* over low heat, beat the chocolate mixture with an electric mixer on low or a rotary mixer for three minutes. Taste and add more cinnamon, if desired. Serve immediately. Serves 4.

The Face That Launched a Thousand Desserts

French chef Marc-Antoine Carême (1784-1833), known as the "king of cooks and the cook of kings," loved to flatter Britain's Princess Charlotte. While in England, he created a lavish pastry which he called the Apple Charlotte, after the lovely lady, and when serving Czar Alexander in Russia, apparently unable to forget the princess, he invented a jellied custard set in a crown of ladyfingers that he named the Charlotte Russe—a delicacy still made in bakeries today.

For Whom the Chips Toll

Here's a story most harried women can relate to—chocolate chip cookies were created in 1933 because innkeeper **Ruth Wakefield** was running late and needed to speed up the process of making cookies. Three years before, she and her husband had bought the Toll House Inn (built in 1709 in Whitman, Massachusetts) and opened a restaurant. That fateful day, she was running late; to save time, she decided that rather than melt chocolate before mixing it into the batter she would simply chop up the hard chocolate and let the bits melt as the cookies baked. The cookies were a huge hit with her customers. At first, Mrs. Wakefield called them chocolate crunch cookies. Later she changed the name to Toll House cookies.

In 1939, Nestle acquired the rights to the Toll House name for an undisclosed sum and began selling the chocolate morsels, and concocting all sorts of

And You Don't Have to Bake Them Yourself

We all love cookies, but who has time to make them? Twenty-one-year-old Californian Debbi Fields, that's who. In 1974, she was smart enough to persuade a Bank of America loan officer that women were getting out of the kitchen and into the boardroom and so there would be a need for fresh-baked commercial cookies. By 1991, there were 800 Mrs. Fields stores around the world; soon after, she sold out to a conglomerate, most likely with enough dough to retire in her forties.

recipes for them. (Straight out of the bag ain't bad either, as many a wild woman can attest.) The recipe, which first appeared in *Ruth Wakefield's Toll House Tried and True Recipes* in 1936, hasn't changed much over the years. Here's Ruth's original—which makes a hundred cookies in one batch. (You wouldn't want a cookie shortage now would you?)

Chocolate Crunch Cookies

1 cup butter

¾ cup brown sugar

¾ cup granulated sugar

2 eggs

1 teaspoon baking soda

1 teaspoon hot water

2¼ cups all-purpose flour

1 teaspoon salt

1 cup chopped nuts

1 pound chocolate chips (16 oz)

1 teaspoon pure vanilla extract

Cream together the butter and sugars. Add the eggs and beat until fluffy. Dissolve the soda in hot water and add to the butter mix. Sift the flour and salt into the mixture and stir well. Add the nuts and chocolate chips and stir. Preheat the oven to 375 degrees. Drop half-teaspoonfuls of dough on a greased cookie sheet and bake 10 to 12 minutes. Makes 100 cookies.

Chocolate Balls

1 cup semisweet chocolate chips

2 tablespoons butter

1 cup powdered sugar

½ teaspoon pure vanilla extract

Why Women Need Chocolate

According to nutritionist Debra Waterhouse, who's just penned a book on the topic, it's perfectly natural for women to crave chocolate. Recent research has shown it's because of estrogen's effects on brain chemicals and blood sugar levels—sugar brings about calmness and mood stability, while fat has mood-elevating effects. Which is why chocolate, with its balance of 50 percent fat and 50 percent sugar, is the perfect female food. Corroborating a biological basis for such choices, researchers asked men and women their three favorite foods, in order of preference. While 67 percent of men said they have no preferred food, the remaining 37 percent chose (1) red meat, (2) pizza, and (3) potatoes. Contrast this with the women's choices: (1) chocolate, (2) bread, and (3) ice cream.

By the way, researchers have also shown that the best way to deal with a craving is to satisfy it immediately with a small portion. Abstinence, they report, only fuels the craving and triggers binges. So go ahead, have a chocolate chip cookie.

2 tablespoons dark rum
½ cup flaked coconut, plus a bit more
½ cup chopped walnuts

In a medium saucepan over low heat, melt the semisweet chocolate chips and butter, stirring frequently. Remove from heat and cool until lukewarm. Then stir in the sugar, vanilla, and rum. Add the coconut and walnuts and mix well. Refrigerate for about 1 hour. Form into 1-inch balls; roll in additional coconut. Place on a plate and chill until firm, about 3 hours. Makes about 2 dozen.

A Rose by Any Other Name

Ever notice how many of the pet names and metaphors for women are based on food? Here are the ones we came up with: "honey," "honey bun," "cream puff," "cheesecake," "muffin," "dumpling," "pumpkin," "sweetie," "sweetie pie," "cutie pie," "cookie," "sweet cookie," "cupcake," "baby cakes," "choux choux," "sugar," "sugar buns," "a chick," "a peach," "a piece of cake," "a honey pot," "a hot tomato," "a hot tamale," "a tart," "a dish," and "sweet enough to eat." Concocted by men, says feminist Brinlee Kramer disapprovingly, they "exemplify the oral fixation men all are subject to." Take that, you guys!

We All Love Lucy

Many of the funniest episodes of this beloved TV series from the fifties involve **Lucy** and food. Who can forget when Lucy stomps grapes, is pinned to the wall by the giant loaf of bread she has over-yeasted, tries to work at the bon-bon factory and ends up eating thousands of pieces of candy, and gets drunk rehearsing the pitch for the cure-all tonic Vitameatavegamin?

When it comes to Lucille Ball's real life in the kitchen, not much is known. However, her ex-husband Desi Arnaz reported that before she became famous, she was once fired as a soda jerk in a New York drugstore because she always forgot to put the bananas in the banana splits. (Perhaps she just didn't like the things).

As long as you don't forget the banana, a banana split can be easily improvised from a banana split lengthwise and topped with two scoops of vanilla ice

cream, a smothering of hot fudge and whipped cream, and a sprinkling of chopped walnuts and a maraschino cherry. However, if your sweet tooth is craving something more exotic, try these toothsome treats.

Caramel Bananas

All-purpose flour

6 firm, ripe bananas, peeled, halved lengthwise, and cut into 2-inch pieces

⅓ cup unsalted butter

½ cup firmly packed brown sugar

½ cup dark rum

Vanilla ice cream

Place the flour in a large shallow dish and roll the bananas in the flour until slightly coated.

In a large, heavy flameproof skillet over medium heat, melt the butter and caramelize the sugar in the butter until golden brown. Add the bananas and sauté for 1 minute. Lower the heat and add the rum. Carefully ignite with a match and cook over low heat until the flames subside. Simmer, stirring frequently, until the sauce thickens, about 3 to 5 minutes. Spoon the bananas and sauce over vanilla ice cream and serve immediately. Serves 6.

Bananas Sabayon

(Nicole Alper)

6 egg yolks

½ cup granulated sugar

1 cup champagne

1 cup cream

2 tablespoons butter

3 large bananas, halved and sliced in 2-inch pieces

½ cup all-purpose flour

2 tablespoons brown sugar

1 cup pecans, toasted and coarsely chopped

Whisk the egg yolks and sugar over a *bain marie* for several minutes, until the mixture starts to thicken. Begin adding the champagne a bit at a time, continuing to whisk. Remove from the *bain marie*. In a separate bowl, beat the cream to soft peaks, then fold it into the egg-yolk mixture.

In a sauté pan, melt the butter. Dip the bananas in the flour and then sauté in the butter. Sprinkle the brown sugar on top and turn continuously in the pan for about 2 minutes.

Have ready 6 serving glasses and put a small scoop of the pecans in the bottom of each glass. Then add several banana slices and top with a generous serving of the sabayon. Serve immediately. Serves 6.

————————— ⬤ —————————

"Bring on the dessert . . . I think I am about to die."
—Pierette, sister of Brillat-Savarin,
shortly before her 100th birthday

Dame Nellie Melba

Nellie Melba was an Australian-born opera singer who made her debut in 1888 at the Brussels Opera singing the role of Gilda in Verdi's *Rigoletto* and quickly became a sensation in the U.S. and Europe. In 1894, she was singing in Wagner's *Lohengrin* at London's Covent Garden and staying at the five-year-old Savoy Hotel, when its well-known chef, August Escoffier, created a special dessert for her. He knew she loved peaches and ice cream, so he topped a cooked peach with a scoop of vanilla ice cream; later he added raspberry purée and almond slivers and called it Peach Melba.

This was not the only food with which Dame Melba was linked. The chef also created, in honor of her appearance in the Puccini opera, Poulard Tosca (which never really caught on). But the soprano is most closely associated with yet another comestible. Always weight-conscious, Melba used to breakfast at the Savoy on tea and bread that Escoffier would grill, then slice and toast again. Thus, her name ultimately came to represent both a low-calorie diet item—Melba Toast—and the decidedly non-dietary dessert.

By the way, to honor other female patrons at a time when respectable women were just beginning to be seen at restaurants, Escoffier also created Soufflé Tetrazzini for Luisa T.; Poulard Belle Hélène for Sarah Bernhardt; and Potage Miss Becky, Salad Naomi, Soufflé Hilda, and Bombe Miss Helyette, among others, for less-well-known ladies. Here we offer Peach Melba and another peach treat.

Peach Melba

2 cups sugar

1 whole vanilla bean

8 peaches, peeled and pitted

2 pints frozen raspberries, thawed

Vanilla ice cream

Slivered almonds

In a large saucepan, bring 1 cup of the sugar and 2 cups of water to a boil, add the vanilla bean, and boil until the syrup reaches 232 degrees on a candy thermometer (thread stage). Add the peaches and cook until they are tender enough to be pierced by a knife, about 15 minutes. Allow to cool slightly.

While the peaches are cooking, combine the raspberries with the remaining cup of sugar and 1 cup water in a small saucepan until thick, then put through a strainer or blender and cool.

In individual serving dishes, put a layer of vanilla ice cream and top with the peaches. Coat with raspberry purée and sprinkle with almonds. Serves 8.

Poached Peaches

2 cups red wine

2 cups water

¼ cup brandy

¼ cup orange juice

2 tablespoons sugar

10 peppercorns

4 cloves

¼ teaspoon allspice

1 bay leaf

1 stick cinnamon

Nobody Doesn't Like Sara Lee

In 1950, Charles Lubin, a Chicago baker, introduced a refrigerated cheesecake, named after his nine-year-old daughter, Sara Lee. The cheesecake proved to be so successful that the kitchens of Sara Lee ultimately became one of the world's largest bakeries. Recently, the cheesecake heiress, now Sara Lee Schupf, proved she wasn't made of whipped cheese—she endowed a professorship for women in science at Skidmore College. She herself is a Skidmore grad, receiving her degree in 1994, thirty-five years after she dropped out and ten years after becoming a trustee of the college.

6 ripe peaches, peeled, halved, and pitted

6 lemon slices

In a large saucepan, combine all ingredients except the peaches and lemon. Bring to a boil, lower the heat, and simmer 5 minutes. Add the peaches and lemon to the pot, cover, and poach on medium-low heat until tender, about 20 minutes. To serve, strain the sauce, place two peach halves in each dessert dish, and spoon the sauce on top. Serves 6.

"While forbidden fruit is said to taste sweeter, it usually spoils faster."
—Abigail Van Buren

Old Bett Lives On

The popular dessert, Apple Brown Betty, got its moniker from pre-Civil War black minstrel shows. The holiday plays contained two characters, Father Christmas and Mother Christmas, who was also known as **Old Bett**. After the performance, Father Christmas would hand out gifts while Old Bett would serve a concoction of dried apples, molasses, and layers of stale bread crumbs.

The concoction really caught on in the United States. There are dozens of variations: with or without molasses, with bread crumbs, with rolled oats, with flour and brown sugar, with other fruits mixed in with the apples. *The Joy of Cooking* even includes a recipe that substitutes ginger snaps for the flour or crumbs. Today these comforting desserts fall under the category of crisps, deep-dish desserts with fruit on the bottom and some kind of crunchy topping baked in the oven.

To be true to Old Bett's recipe, we offer a bread-crumb-topping version as well as one made with rolled oats. But because tastes have changed over the years, we replace the molasses with brown sugar.

Apple Brown Betty

1 lemon

¼ cup brown sugar

¼ teaspoon nutmeg

¼ teaspoon cinnamon

5 large tart apples, peeled, cored, and thinly sliced

4 tablespoons butter

5 slices whole wheat bread, broken into tiny pieces

Cream or milk, optional

Preheat the oven to 350 degrees. Grate the lemon and combine the zest, sugar, nutmeg, and cinnamon in a small bowl. Set aside. Squeeze the lemon juice over the apples to keep them from turning brown. Melt 2 tablespoons of the butter and combine with the bread in a medium bowl. Set aside.

Grease a 2-quart baking dish. Place a third of the crumbs in the bottom of the dish and cover with half of the apples and ½ of the sugar-lemon zest mixture. Repeat for a second layer and end with the remaining bread crumbs. Dot the top with the remaining 2 tablespoons of butter.

Bake, covered, for 35 to 40 minutes, then remove the cover and bake for an additional 10 to 15 minutes, or until the top is browned and the fruit is bubbly. Serve warm, with cream or milk if desired. Serves 6.

Cranberry Apple Crisp

½ cup rolled oats

½ cup plus 3 tablespoons all-purpose flour

⅓ cup packed dark brown sugar

¼ cup butter, cut into small pieces

4 large Granny Smith Apples, peeled, cored, and thinly sliced

1 cup cranberries

¼ to ½ cup sugar, depending on how tart you like it

½ teaspoon ground cinnamon

¼ teaspoon ground nutmeg

Preheat the oven to 350 degrees. Grease a 13x9x2-inch baking pan.

In a small bowl, combine the oats, ½ cup of the flour, and brown sugar. Add the butter and combine with fingers until crumbly.

In a large bowl, toss the apples, cranberries, sugar, the remaining 2 tablespoons flour, cinnamon, and nutmeg. Pour this mixture into the greased pan and crumble the oat mixture over the fruit. Bake, uncovered, until the apples are tender, about 1¼ hours. Serves 4.

Another Enterprising Female

Marie Callender, who died in 1995 at the age of eighty-eight, offers a typical rags-to-riches story. She began her career making pies at home during World War II, selling them to a local deli. In 1948, she set up shop in a rented Quonset™ hut and started wider distribution. By 1986, when she sold out to Ramada Inn, her Marie Callender's Restaurants & Bakeries had sales of one hundred seventy-five million dollars.

A Divine Dining Companion

L illian Russell (1861–1922) was a famous burlesque and Broadway musical singer known as much for her curves as for her chords. "To writer Edna Ferber," writes Autumn Stephens in *Wild Women,* "the famous full-blown figure of diva Lillian Russell resembled a roller coaster. To a more poetically minded critic from the *New York World,* the undulating curves were 'so many sonnets of motion.' But to most Americans in the latter two decades of the nineteenth century, rotund Russell—the most photographed woman of her generation—simply represented the epitome of female beauty.

"Ill-suited to the role of Victorian shrinking violet, Russell reveled in a lifestyle as flamboyant as the lush lines of her body suggested. In an era when a rare glimpse of feminine ankle sent male minds reeling, she mounted the stage in scandalously short skirts, her sturdy legs showcased in purple tights. Indifferent to the stares of strangers, she rolled through Central Park on a gold-plated bicycle, its spokes studded with diamonds, rubies, and emeralds. And in 1890, her well-known voice was the first to waft over the new long-distance wires, warbling an operatic arai into the far-off ear of President Benjamin Harrison.

"Naturally, a nation that worshipped at the altar of Russell's avoirdupois hungered to know her beauty secrets. Obligingly, the press reported that the gorgeous gourmande (an Iowa girl born and bred) liked nothing better for lunch than a platter of corn on the cob followed by crêpes suzette. Her solution to the dessert dilemma was duly noted: she chose both cantaloupe and ice cream. And it was a proud day for fans of feminine flesh when she challenged outrageously outsized Diamond Jim Brady (who was known for eating six meals a day) to a conspicuous consumption contest, and matched him bite for bite."

Old Lil spent as little time as possible in the kitchen—she had others do her cooking—but we thought honoring such an eater calls for a crêpes suzette recipe, as well as other sinful sensations.

Crêpes Suzette

Filling

1 very ripe pear

1 tablespoon currant jelly

1 tablespoon butter, melted

½ lemon, juiced, or 4 teaspoons lemon juice

1 tablespoon sugar

¼ teaspoon pure vanilla extract

½ teaspoon grated lemon peel

1 tablespoon white curaçao

---

2 tablespoons butter, melted

1 tablespoon all-purpose flour

1 tablespoon milk

1 egg, beaten

1 teaspoon sugar

6 tablespoons brandy (optional)

Peel and core the pear, removing any brown spots. In a medium bowl, mash the pear with a fork. Add the other filling ingredients and mix well. Set aside while you make the crêpes.

Put melted butter into the bottom of a shallow, heatproof serving dish and set in a warm spot by the stove. In a small bowl, combine the flour and milk and stir until lump-free; add the egg and mix well again.

Heat a small frying pan over medium-high heat until drop of butter bounces across the surface. Brush the frying pan with melted butter from the serving dish. Pour ¼ of the batter into the pan and swiftly swirl it to just coat the surface. (It should be a very thin pancake.) When it begins to puff in the middle, quickly turn it over. Remove the crêpe from the pan and spread it with ¼ of the filling, roll it up, and place it in the serving dish. Keep it hot while you repeat the process 3 times.

Sprinkle the rolled crêpes with granulated sugar. If using the brandy, warm it in a small skillet, then ignite it with a match. When the flames subside, pour it over the crêpes. Serves 2.

Quatre Quart

(This happens to be a favorite of Nicole's Parisian mother, in whose honor it is given here.)

4 eggs

Butter

Sugar

All-purpose flour

½ teaspoon baking powder

½ teaspoon baking soda

5 red plums, sliced (optional)

Powdered sugar

A Quatre Quart is a traditional French pound cake made of 4 equal parts. In order to determine the amount of butter, sugar, and flour, weigh the 4 eggs. Then weigh the other ingredients so that each equals the weight of the eggs.

Preheat the oven to 350 degrees. In a bowl, combine all ingredients except the powdered sugar until smooth. Pour the batter into a buttered and floured bundt pan. Bake for about 50 minutes, until the top is brown and a toothpick inserted in the center comes out clean. Turn the cake out onto a wire rack and cool. Dust with powdered sugar before serving. Serves 12.

No More Mom in the Apron?

According to a recent marketing survey, retail sales of products for home baking are declining, because women are just too busy to bake. Either they are working full time and raising a family, or working part time, raising a family, and looking for more work. (The idea that men might pitch in in the cookie department apparently didn't occur to the researchers.) Yet 63.3 percent of the women surveyed still make cookies from scratch, 38.6 percent still make their own pies (including the crusts!), and 38.1 percent still make biscuits from scratch.

Cooking with Alice

Alice B. Toklas was thirty when she met avant-garde writer, modern art collector, and self-proclaimed genius Gertrude Stein in Paris in 1907. She knew Stein's family in California and had been urged to look Gert up when she arrived in France. Thus began a thirty-seven-year relationship. Quicker than you can say "true love," lovely Alice moved in with the writer and her brother at 27 rue de Fleurs, and the two women set about wining and dining everyone in Paris who was anyone in modern art or literature between the two world wars. Regulars included artists Picasso (who painted Gertrude's portrait), Matisse, and Braque, as well as writers Ernest Hemingway and Sherwood Anderson. Theirs was a harmonious set-up: Alice would whip up meals in the kitchen while Gertrude held forth in the living room—and it was a toss-up as to which attracted the visitors more. Toklas was a fabulous cook—and many of the artists were starving, at least at first.

In 1933, *The Autobiography of Alice B. Toklas* was published, a witty revelation that was actually written by Gertrude as if it were Alice writing about Gertrude and their adventures together—a very Steinian literary device. "Channeling" Alice was apparently good for Gertrude—the "autobiography" was definitely her most coherent piece of writing and the only one of her books to reach a wide audience. Indeed, when pressed for an autobiography of her own, Alice used the excuse that there already was one, and she never did reveal her side of the love story. Instead she penned *The Alice B. Toklas Cookbook* in 1954.

It caused a minor sensation at the time because it contains a recipe for haschish fudge, "the food of Paradise . . . which anyone could whip up on a rainy day" (although she conceded that "[o]btaining the *canibus* may present certain difficulties"). In M.F.K. Fisher's foreword to a more recent edition of the cookbook, Fisher, who knew Alice well, notes that Alice was famous for such daring items, but that they looked more like fudge brownies and, although Fisher had never tasted them herself, they were reputed to be quite bitter—and to either have no effect or be quite lethal—depending on how much herb was included. Alice attributes the recipe—which is not our idea of fudge at all, but a mixture of chopped dried fruits and nuts—to a friend, Brion Gysin, although the rumored version of how Alice came to make it is more juicy. Supposedly, Alice was in the kitchen one day whipping up some fudge when in walked writer Paul Bowles, who handed her some crumbled-up hash and told her it was a new spice. Alice mixed it in and they all had a very nice time.

Exactly however, wherever, and whatever may never be known, but what we do know makes for a great story. Unfortunately, it does not make for a good recipe, so we've decided to offer a substitute, in the fudge spirit. But first, lest you feel cheated, here's the original; you be the judge.

Haschich Fudge
(From *The Alice B. Toklas Cookbook*)

Take 1 teaspoon black peppercorns, 1 whole nutmeg, 4 average sticks of cinnamon, 1 teaspoon coriander. These should all be pulverized in a mortar. About a handful each of stoned [pitted] dates, dried figs, shelled almonds and peanuts: chop these and mix them together. A bunch of cannabis sativa can be pulverized. This along with the spices should be dusted over the mixed fruit and nuts, kneaded together. [Add] about a cup of sugar dissolved in a big pat of butter. Rolled into a cake and cut into pieces or made into balls about the size of a walnut, it should be eaten with care. Two pieces are often quite sufficient."

Chocolate Fudge Tart
(by Lynette Rohrer)

Caramel

1 cup sugar
2½ ounces ground coffee

———————

2 ounces semi-sweet chocolate
½ ounce unsweetened chocolate

Ohh FUDGE!!

Sensational starlet and bobbed extraordinaire Louise Brooks was as passionate about her fudge as she was about her naughty nocturnal activities. Willing to go to great lengths to hoard her gooey chocolate delicacy, which she made herself, this insouciant autodidact would often spit on every piece of fudge in the pan to prevent anyone else from eating it!

3 ounces butter

2 eggs

⅓ cup all-purpose flour

1 prebaked pie crust or tart shell

First make the caramel. In a small heavy saucepan, caramelize the sugar in 2 ounces of water until golden brown. Add the coffee and remove from the heat.

Preheat the oven to 350 degrees. In a heavy saucepan, melt together the two chocolates and the butter over medium heat. Then beat in the eggs, the flour, and the caramel. Pour into the prepared crust and bake until set and a knife inserted in the center comes out clean, about 40 minutes. Serves 8.

Tamer and Truer Fudge

Emelyn Hartridge was no Alice B., merely a student at Vassar trying to make ends meet, when she began to sell fudge out of her dorm room and inadvertently became the first person to realize the candy's commercial value. Previously, fudge was seen as a mistake resulting from either overcooking fondant or undercooking caramel. The chocolate fudge Emelyn sold proved so popular that Vassar soon put fudge kitchens in every dorm. (What that did to Emelyn's business was not recorded.) Not surprisingly, fudge-making also spread to the other colleges in the area and from there out into the world at large.

Women's Illustrious Cookbook Careers

Women and cookbooks just seem to go together. The first American cookbook was *American Cookery, or the Art of Dressing Viands, Fish, Poultry, and Vegetables, and the Best Modes of Making Pastes, Puffs, Pies, Tarts, Cakes, from the Imperial Plumb to Plain Cake Adapted to This Country & All Grades of Life,* published in 1796 by Amelia Simmons, a self-proclaimed orphan. Her aim, she claimed, was to improve "the rising generation of females in America," particularly of orphans. "If orphans pay some attention to cooking they will be welcome wherever they are, and may even attract husbands," advised Ms. Simmons.

Orphans aside, the 47-page cookbook proved extremely popular, going through four editions. "Previously, American women had to rely on English cookbooks which often called for ingredients which were often unavailable in the colonies," writes Peter Stevens in *The Mayflower Murderer & Other Forgotten Firsts in American History.* "*American Cookery* included, for the first time, recipes for such colonial dishes as Indian slapjacks, pumpkin pie, corn bread, and roasted wild turkey, and used American colloquialisms such as *cookie, shortening, slaw* for salad, and squash." (By the way, if you happen onto a copy, hold onto it for dear life—originally sold for three pence, a first edition is reputed to be worth nearly nine thousand dollars today.)

Success always breeds imitators and the success of this book proved no exception. In 1808, one Miss Lucy Emerson came out with *The New England Cookery, or the Art of Dressing all Kinds of Flesh, Fish, and Vegetables, and the Best Modes of Making Pastes, Puffs, Pies, Tarts, Puddings, Custards, and Preserves, and*

All Kinds of Cakes, from the Imperial Plum to Plain Cake (notice any similarity so far?). Lazy Lucy not only helped herself to many of Amelia's recipes, she pilfered the introduction as well and even claimed to be an orphan, too.

On a more legitimate note, the subsequent English cookbook that hit it big was Eliza Acton's *Modern Cookery for Private Families,* published in 1845. Eliza really wanted to be a poet, but her publisher convinced her that there was no market for poems by maiden ladies, but there was one for a good sensible cookery book. She took his advice, which proved to be sound—the book was a classic for years.

The next woman to fire a salvo in the cookbook wars was Britain's Isabella Mary Beeton. In 1861, she brought out *Household Management,* a three-pound, 1,296-page cookery bible. What inspired Mrs. Beeton to put pen to paper, as she wrote in the foreword, "was the discomfort and suffering brought on upon men and women by household mismanagement. I have always thought that there is no more fruitful source of family discontent than a housewife's badly cooked dinners and untidy ways. Men are so well served out of doors—in their well-ordered taverns and dining places—that in order to compete with the attraction of these places, a mistress must be thoroughly acquainted with the theory and practice of cookery."

The tome was a bestseller for over fifty years, with more than a half-million copies sold. Whether Isabella put a dent in pub attendance, however, is unclear. What is more obvious is that she set off a trend that continues unabated to date: the authorship, by women, of more and more of the influential cookbooks. Here we offer some toothsome desserts inspired by Amelia Simmons' recipes, but adapted to modern tastes and techniques.

Pumpkin Pudding

(By Lynette Rohrer)

4 cups milk

2 cups cornmeal

2 cups pumpkin purée

4 eggs

1 cup molasses

1 teaspoon ground allspice

2 teaspoons ground ginger

1 cup cream

Whipped cream (optional)

Preheat the oven to 350 degrees. In a large saucepan over medium-low heat, combine milk and cornmeal and heat until thickened. Add the pumpkin, eggs, molasses, allspice, and ginger, and stir well. Remove from the heat and pour into a casserole dish. Pour the 1 cup cream on top and cover with aluminum foil. Bake for ½ hour, then stir in the cream; replace the cover and bake for an additional ½ hour. Serve with whipped cream, if desired. Serves 8.

Pumpkin Custard Pie

1 unbaked pie crust

1 tablespoon milk

1 tablespoon plus ½ cup sugar

1 16-ounce can solid pack pumpkin

1 cup sour cream

½ cup whipping cream

½ cup golden brown sugar, firmly packed

2 large eggs

1 teaspoon ground cinnamon

1 teaspoon ground ginger

¼ teaspoon ground cloves

¼ teaspoon salt

½ cup sugar

1 cup chilled whipping cream

⅓ cup powdered sugar

Position a rack in the bottom third of the oven and preheat to 350 degrees. Line the crust with foil. Fill with dried beans or pie weights. Bake until the sides are just set, about 15 minutes. Remove the foil and beans and bake until the crust is pale golden, about 12 minutes. If the crust bubbles up, pierce it with a fork. Transfer to a rack; cool.

While the crust is cooking, in a large bowl whisk together the pumpkin, sour cream, ½ cup whipping cream, brown sugar, eggs, cinnamon, ginger, nutmeg, cloves, salt, and ½ cup sugar until well blended. Pour into the prepared crust. Bake until the filling puffs around the edges and the center is almost set, about 55 minutes. Transfer to a rack and cool completely.

Whip the chilled whipping cream with the powdered sugar until stiff peaks form. Serve the pie topped with whipped cream. Serves 8.

Molasses Gingerbread

1¼ cups all-purpose flour

1 teaspoon baking soda

2 teaspoons ground ginger

1¼ teaspoons ground cardamom

¼ teaspoon ground cinnamon

¼ teaspoon ground cloves

¼ teaspoon salt

1 stick butter, room temperature

½ cup brown sugar, firmly packed

1 egg

1 cup unsulfured molasses

½ cup boiling water

Preheat the oven to 350 degrees. Grease a 9-inch-round cake pan and set aside.

Sift all the dry ingredients into a medium bowl. In a large bowl, using an electric mixer, cream the butter, then add the sugar and eggs, and beat until fluffy. Gradually add molasses and mix until well combined. Add the dry ingredients and mix on low. Add the boiling water and stir.

Pour the batter into the pan and bake until a toothpick inserted in the center comes out clean, about 30 minutes. Cool completely on a wire rack before inverting onto a plate. Serves 8.

Stuffed Apples

1 cup currants

1 cup sherry

4 medium baking apples, such as Rome Beauty

2 whole cinnamon sticks, broken in half

Put the currants in a small bowl and pour the sherry over them. Let soak while you core and peel the apples.

Other Beloved Cookbooks by Women

Fannie Merritt Farmer: *Boston Cooking School Cook Book* (1896)

Myrna Johnston: *Better Homes and Gardens New Cook Book* (1930)

Irma Rombauer: *The Joy of Cooking* (1931)

Julia Child: *Mastering the Art of French Cooking* (1961)

Carol Flinders: *Laurel's Kitchen* (1976)

Molly Katzen: *The Moosewood Cookbook* (1977)

Sheila Lukins and Julee Russo: *The Silver Palate Cookbook* (1982)

Alice Waters: *The Chez Panisse Menu Cookbook* (1982)

Martha Stewart: *The Martha Stewart Cookbook* (1995)

Drain the currants, reserving the sherry. Arrange the apples in a microwaveable dish and stuff the currants into them. Insert a cinnamon stick into each apple and pour the reserved sherry into the bottom of the dish. Cover with plastic and microwave on high until the apples are tender, about 8 minutes. Serves 4.

Unforgettable Feminine Food Movie Scenes

- The "I'll never go hungry again" speech in *Gone with the Wind*
- The fig scene in *Women in Love*
- Dinner in *Tom Jones*
- Meg heating up the deli in *When Harry Met Sally*
- Diane torturing Woody with lobsters in *Annie Hall*
- Richard stuffing strawberries and everything else he can get ahold of into Kim's eager mouth in *Nine and and a Half Weeks*
- The scene in *The Little Mermaid* in which the crab has a tête à tête with the chef, who chases him around the kitchen
- The many banquets in *The Age of Innocence* at which Michelle Pfeiffer's character is simultaneously honored and shunned

Top It Off with a Great Cake

*I*n the pre-Civil War South, wedding banquets and other grand events were often topped off with the ultimate cooking challenge of the day, "A Great Cake." A recipe for such a cake is found in Mrs. Colquitt's *Savannah Cook Book,* which "was copied from an old manuscript dated Mt. Vernon, 1781. It calls for 40 eggs, 4 pounds of butter (creamed), 4 pounds of sugar, 5 pounds of flour, and 5 pounds of fruit," according to Kathleen Ann Smallzried in *The Everlasting Pleasure: Influences on America's Kitchens, Cooks and Cookery, from 1565 to the Year 2000.* "This sounds quite daunting," reminds Ms. Smallzried, "until you consider that in 1850 Miss Mary Deas Ravenel's *Carolina Housewife* gives a Great Cake recipe . . . that calls for 20 pounds of butter, flour, sugar, raisins, nutmegs, 20 glasses of wine and brandy, 40 pounds of currants. It vaguely calls for 10 eggs to the pound, which if interpreted to mean to the pounds of batter, would mean 1,500 eggs!"

Just how many mouths such cakes would typically feed is not revealed, but it is important to remember that the women actually creaming, beating, and chopping for these grandiose creations were slaves—Scarlett and her friends wouldn't have been caught dead in the kitchen. Which helps explain why the practice has gone out of style: no one would willingly torture themselves in this fashion. We offer instead a couple of recipes that don't require nearly as much work.

Blueberry Coconut Cake

2 cups self-rising flour

1 cup sugar

1 stick butter, cut into pieces

⅔ cup lightly toasted shredded coconut

½ cup coconut milk

2 eggs

1 teaspoon pure vanilla extract

1 21-ounce can blueberry pie filling

1 tablespoon lemon juice

Preheat the oven to 325 degrees. Grease a 13x9x2-inch baking pan. Combine the flour and sugar in a large bowl. Add the butter and mix with fingers until crumbly. Transfer ½ cup of this mixture to a small bowl, stir in the coconut, and set aside for topping.

To the flour mixture in the large bowl, add the coconut milk, eggs, and vanilla, beating after each addition until well combined. Pour the batter into the prepared baking pan.

Combine the blueberry filling and lemon juice, and spread over the batter. Sprinkle the topping evenly over all. Bake until a toothpick inserted into the center comes out clean, about 45 minutes. Cool on a rack. Serves 8.

Chocolate Cupcakes

(By Lynette Rohrer)

⅓ cup all-purpose flour

6 ounces sugar

2 eggs plus 1 yolk

3½ ounces butter

3 ounces semisweet chocolate

A pinch of salt

Combine the flour and sugar in a large bowl. Add the eggs and the extra yolk, and beat until smooth.

In a small heavy saucepan over medium-low heat, melt the butter and chocolate together with the salt. Remove from heat and combine with the flour mixture. Refrigerate for 3 hours.

Preheat the oven to 375 degrees. Scoop the batter into greased cupcake tins and bake until a toothpick inserted in the center comes out clean, about 20 minutes. Makes 1 dozen cup cakes.

A Peach of a Woman

It is traditional for the Shakers to commemorate the birthday of their founder, Ann Lee (1736–1784), known by all as Mother Ann, by holding an afternoon meeting followed by supper, at which Mother Ann's Birthday Cake is served. The original recipe advises: "Cut a handful of peach twigs which are filled with sap at this season of the year (February). Clip the ends and bruise them and beat the cake batter with them. This will impart a delicate peach flavor to the cake."

We All Scream for Ice Cream

When it comes to ice cream, women have always been in the picture. When she married King Henri II in 1533, Catherine de Medici, that Johnny Appleseed of Italian food, used fruit ices to demonstrate her country's culinary sophistication to the rest of Europe. During the month-long nuptials, her confectioners served a different flavored ice every day, including lemon, lime, orange, cherry, and wild strawberry. She also served a semi-frozen dessert made from thick, sweetened cream, the precursor to modern ice cream.

A century later, the first ice cream known in England was consumed at Windsor Castle. (Boy, does it take those royals a long time to break with tradition!) The first sighting of ice cream in the United States was in 1744. Thomas Jefferson made a type of French sorbet while president and served it at a White House dinner in 1803. But it wasn't until 1813, when James Madison was sworn in as the fourth president and his wife Dolley served it at the inaugural party, that ice cream began to catch on in earnest. That act by darling Dol certainly made history—it is the only item about her in *The Women's Chronology*.

One reason for the low consumption of ice cream was lack of proper equipment. But in 1846, Philadelphia dairymaid Nancy Johnson fixed that: She invented the first portable hand-cranked ice cream freezer, in which a churn beat the mixture of cream and flavoring with a paddle as the mixture froze. The invention revolutionized ice cream production, enabling anyone who bought it to produce high-quality ice cream at home. Whether Nancy got rich off of her invention is unknown.

Nowadays, electric ice cream makers take even more work out of making your own. But still, most folks have the store-bought variety.

Crème Fraîche Ice Cream
(Tastes like cheesecake, says Lynette)

6 cups crème fraîche

1½ cups sugar

16 egg yolks

In a medium saucepan over medium-low heat, heat the crème fraîche. Meanwhile, whip eggs and sugar together in a bowl. Pour half of the warm créme fraîche into the egg mixture, then pour this mixture into the rest of the crème fraîche in the saucepan. Cook over low heat for about 3 minutes, then chill in an ice bath for about twenty minutes until cool. Then freeze in an ice cream freezer according to manufacturer's directions. Makes 2 quarts.

Baked Alaska

1 quart brick-style-box ice cream, any flavor

*1 1-inch-thick slab of sponge or layer cake, at least
1 inch longer and wider than the ice cream*

5 egg whites

1 teaspoon pure vanilla extract

½ teaspoon cream of tartar

⅔ cup sugar

Measure length and width of ice cream and if necessary trim cake to 1 inch larger on all sides. Place the cake on a piece of aluminum foil and center the ice cream on the cake. Cover and freeze till firm, about 1 hour.

At serving time, place the oven rack on the lowest setting and preheat the oven to 500 degrees. In a medium bowl, using an electric mixer, beat together the egg whites, vanilla, and cream of tartar until the mixture forms soft peaks. Gradually add the sugar until the meringue forms stiff peaks.

Remove the cake and ice cream from the freezer and place them on a baking sheet. Spread the meringue over the ice cream, being sure to cover completely down to the edges of the cake. Bake 3 minutes or until the meringue is golden brown. Serve immediately. Serves 8.

Cone Creations

A woman was also behind the ice cream cone. In 1904, one Charles E. Menches was employed by an ice cream manufacturer in St. Louis, Missouri. Being a romantic kind of guy, he frequently took ice cream sandwiches and flowers to his girlfriend after work. One day this anonymous lass couldn't find a vase for the flowers, so she rolled one layer of the ice cream sandwich into a cone to act as a vase. Then she rolled the other layer into a cone, scooping the ice cream into that one. The ice cream cone was invented! (By the way, this fanciful story is untrue, according to *The Food Chronology*. It did happen in St. Louis, but it was at the World Exposition, and the baker was a Syrian pastry maker who improvised a cone for a nearby ice cream stand that had run out of dishes. Or else it was Italo Marchiony, who claimed to have a patent on a cone machine since 1896. But we're sticking to our story.)

Frieda's Finest

*I*f you are an aficionado of fresh papayas, pineapples, passion fruit, blood oranges, kiwis, raddicchio, sunchokes, jicama, chayote, pearl onions, spaghetti squash, or sugar snap peas, give thanks to **Frieda Caplan**, who in the early sixties introduced these delicacies—and many others—into American kitchens. Frieda was a Los Angeles businesswoman who hit upon the idea of importing exotic fresh fruits and vegetables from around the world and selling them to U.S. stores. But this innovative marketer realized that she must first create a market for such items—otherwise, they'd just rot on the shelves. So she gave away free samples to influential food editors and produce buyers (she even had a restaurant chef invent kiwi tarts) to ensure shelf space and publicity, and marketed all her items with recipes attached, ensuring that consumers would know what to do with them when they got home.

Soon, this 39-year-old dynamo brought her two daughters, Karen and Jackie, into the business and built Frieda's into a 23-million-dollar-a-year business, currently selling over 500 items—with an all-woman sales force. In honor of this accomplishment, we present two desserts featuring some items that Frieda made popular.

Tropical Fruit Coupe

1½ cups dry white wine

½ cup sugar

1 vanilla bean, split lengthwise

½ cup chopped fresh mint

½ small ripe pineapple, peeled, cored, and cubed

1 small ripe papaya, peeled and cubed

2 oranges or blood oranges, sectioned

3 cups fresh blueberries, washed

½ honeydew melon, cubed

In a small saucepan, combine ½ cup of the wine and the sugar. Add the vanilla bean. Stir over low heat until the sugar is dissolved and the syrup is very hot, about 2 minutes. Remove from the heat, steep for 30 minutes, and then remove the bean. Add the remaining wine and the mint.

In a large bowl, combine all the fruit. Pour the syrup over the fruit, cover, and refrigerate for at least 1 hour. Serve in goblets with a bit of syrup spooned on top. Serves 6.

Kiwi & Mango Delight

2 kiwis

2 mangoes

1 cup sugar

1 teaspoon almond extract

Slice the kiwis in ⅓-inch slices. Dice the mangoes and mix together. In a small saucepan, heat the sugar with 1 cup water until dissolved. Add the almond extract and cool. Drizzle the syrup over the fruit. Serves 4.

Passionate Punches and Creative Cocktails

Of Babes and Brewskis

Beer was the drink of choice in ancient Mesopotamia (present-day Iraq), land of the Sumerians and other ancient civilizations. They were such beer-swillers that one Greek legend says Dionysus, the Greek god of wine, ran from Mesopotamia in disgust because the inhabitants were so addicted to beer.

The Sumerians loved their suds so much they even had a slogan, "Beer makes the liver happy and fills the heart with joy." There was a reasonable rationale for their enthusiasm, however, for in ancient times, water was likely to make you sick. Thick barley beer, on the other hand, was relatively germ-free and nourishing too.

Most of the Sumerian brewers were women who made beer at home and sold it in taverns. Indeed, the industry was so female-dominated that the famous law code drawn up by the Babylonian king Hammurabi about 1,750 B.C. specified that women who overcharged for beer should be thrown in the river as punishment.

One such woman, writes Vicki León in *Uppity Women of Ancient Times,* was "Kubaba, a sharp and sturdy lady who kept a tavern in the Sumerian city of Kish (located about fifty-five miles south of modern Baghdad). Then as now, taverns had reputations for rowdiness, rigged prices, and watered drinks . . . .

"Kubaba had higher ambitions than pulling drafts and running the local version of Cheers. With the possible help of some beer-oriented campaign promises, she managed to become queen of Kish, gaining the throne about 2,500 B.C. No splash-in-the-beer-barrel, one-term ruler, Kubaba rose to highest prominence and stayed there. Her sons succeeded her, and the dynasty she founded lasted for one hundred years."

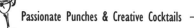

In honor of this feisty woman, we offer the following beer concoction, more commonly know as a Brown Betty. It's perfect for a cold winter's night.

Kubaba's Kiss

½ cup brown sugar

1 lemon, sliced

4 whole cloves

1 cinnamon stick

¼ teaspoon grated nutmeg

¼ teaspoon ground ginger

2¼ cups water

12 ounces (1½ cups) brandy

4 (12-ounce) bottles amber ale, such as Bass™

Over medium-high heat, combine the brown sugar, lemon slices, cloves, cinnamon stick, nutmeg, ginger, and water in a large nonreactive pan. Stir frequently until sugar is dissolved. Let the mixture come to a boil, turn the heat down to medium, and simmer for 10 minutes. Add the brandy and ale, and heat but do not allow to come to a boil. Serve in beer mugs, garnished with a lemon slice. Serves 8.

"There comes a time in every woman's life when the only thing that helps is a glass of champagne."

—Bette Davis

Women to Wet Your Whistle

Who thinks up the names for mixed drinks? Given the preponderance of male bartenders, we could hazard a guess. While perusing *The Bartender's Bible,* we found, besides the usual quantity of flips, swizzles, smashes, and fizzes, a great number of female-inspired cocktails. After listing them all, we saw they fell into certain categories. Most have sexual overtones, but then there's Betsy Ross.

The Femme Fatales: Widow Woods Nightcap, Sandra Buys a Dog, Trouble for Tina, Zultry Zoe, Hot Zultry Zoe, Hillary Wallbanger, Brooke Shields (nonalcoholic, of course), and Betsy Rosses 1 and 2

The Various Belles: Southern Belle, Miss Belle, Belles of St. Mary's, Belle of Ellis Island

Items of Clothing: Grass Skirt, Hot Pants, Petticoat Lane, Silk Stocking

Body Parts: Witch's Tit, Bosom Caresser, Damn-Your-Eyes

The Female Life Cycle as Seen Through Certain Male Eyes: Maiden's Blush, Pretty Thing, Dirty Girl Scout, Maiden-no-More, Brazen Hussy, Bitch-on-Wheels, Shady Lady, Merry Widow, Widow with a Secret

A Male Fantasy: Evans Rescues the Damsel of Garstang Tower (honest!)

The Three-Hundred-Dollar Coke Habit

Heiress **Christina Onassis** was eccentric, to say the least. She seldom arose before 3:00 P.M., when she would breakfast on a chocolate croissant and a Diet Coke™, which she referred to as "my one-calorie tipple." In *Heiress: The Story of Christina Onassis,* Nigel Dempster tells of the lengths to which Onassis was willing to go to stay in stock.

At the time, Diet Coke™ was not available in France, where Onassis lived; therefore "each week Christina's ten-seater jet was dispatched to New York to bring back precisely one hundred bottles. 'Why not a thousand bottles?' Yves asked Hélène (head waiter and chief housekeeper, respectively, at Christina's apartment on Avenue Foch in Paris).

"'Because Madame doesn't want old Diet Coke™,' Hélène explained, and suggested that he serve it with considerable respect since it worked out at three hundred dollars a bottle."

You can make the following with Diet or Classic Coke™; either way it is guaranteed not to be as extravagantly priced.

"One more drink and I'd have been under the host."
—Dorothy Parker

Cuba Libre

2 ounces light rum

5 ounces cola

1 lime wedge

Pour the rum and cola into a highball glass almost filled with ice cubes. Stir well. Garnish with the lime. Serves 1.

Effective, If Expensive, Dieting Method

The unquestioned sovereign of New York society, Caroline Astor hosted the most extravagant dinners and balls of the nineteenth century until her death at seventy-seven in 1908. "On one occasion," writes Douglas Meldrum in *The Night 2000 Men Came to Dinner,* "she covered her dinner table with several inches of sand in which she buried diamonds, sapphires, rubies, and emeralds. At each place setting there was a small sterling silver bucket with a spade to help guests 'dig for treasure.'"

Liz's Chocolate Indulgence

When it came to imbibing both food and drink, **Elizabeth Taylor**, in her heyday, was second to none. In her autobiography, the lovely Liz tells the following tale from her raucous drinking days. During the making of *Giant*, she said, "Rock [Hudson] and I hit it off right away and acted like a pair of kids. During our toots, we concocted the best drink I ever tasted—a chocolate martini made with vodka, Hershey's™ syrup, and Kahlua™. How we survived, I'll never know."

Liz's memory for exactly how such a brew was concocted is hazy to say the least, and you're probably not interested in a chocolate syrup martini anyway. However, if you're feeling particularly adventurous, you might want to play around with the chocolate idea—and let us know if you hit upon the right combination.

The Classic Martini

2½ ounces gin

1½ teaspoons dry vermouth

1 lemon twist or 1 cocktail olive

Fill a mixing glass half full with ice cubes, then add the gin and vermouth. Stir or shake well. (Whether the perfect martini is to be stirred or shaken is a matter of great controversy—use your own judgment.) Strain into a cocktail glass and garnish with a lemon twist or olive, your choice. Serves 1.

Martini Cooler

1½ ounces gin

1 teaspoon dry vermouth

4 ounces lemon-lime soda

1 lemon twist

Fill a highball glass ¾ full with ice cubes. Add the gin, vermouth, and soda. Stir well. Garnish with the lemon twist. Serves 1.

"As with most fine things, chocolate has its season. There is a simple memory aid that you can use to determine whether it is the correct time to order chocolate dishes; Any month whose name contains the letter a, e, or u is the proper time for chocolate."

—Sandra Boynton

The Truth Is in the Tea

In 1943, at the height of World War II, President and Mrs. Roosevelt invited Madame Chiang Kai-shek of China to tea at the White House. Wanting to make a good impression, Mrs. Roosevelt had secured some very special 100-year-old Chinese tea. When their guest sipped the tea daintily without comment, Mrs. Roosevelt couldn't resist telling her about it. "In my country, tea kept so long is used only for medicinal purposes," replied Madame Chiang.

Indeed, tea has many uses in Asia. In Tibet, which is extremely mountainous, massive amounts of tea are given to horses and mules to increase their capacity to work, and the distance between villages, according to William Emboden in *Narcotic Plants*, is calculated by the number of cups of tea necessary to sustain someone traveling between them. He says, "It has been ascertained that three cups of tea is equal to eight kilometers."

The following punches do call for tea, but the fresher the better and given their quantity of alcohol they probably won't have you gamboling up mountains. Well, then again...

Sunset Punch

2 cups lemon juice

1 cup superfine sugar

2 750-ml bottles chilled champagne

6 ounces maraschino liqueur

8 ounces Cointreau™

3 ounces cherry brandy

3 ounces brandy

2 cups tea, chilled

1 block of ice

2 oranges, cut into slices

24 maraschino cherries

Stir the lemon juice and sugar together in a large punch bowl until the sugar is dissolved. Add the remaining liquids, and stir well. Add the ice and garnish with the orange slices and the cherries. Makes enough for twenty-two 6-ounce punch cups.

Red Wine Punch

2 cups lemon juice

1 cup superfine sugar

3 750-ml bottles dry red wine

1½ cups brandy

½ cup apricot brandy

½ cup bourbon

1 cup Cointreau™ or triple sec

1 quart club soda

2 cups cold tea

1 block of ice

3 oranges cut into slices

Stir the lemon juice and sugar together in a large punch bowl until the sugar is dissolved. Add the remaining liquids and stir well. Add the ice and garnish with the orange slices. Makes enough for thirty 6-ounce punch cups.

Tiny Bubbles

- Madame de Pompadour, mistress of Louis XV, described champagne as "the only wine that leaves a woman beautiful after drinking it."

- Napoleon Bonaparte didn't touch the stuff, but Empress Josephine did. She ran up such champagne bills that it became an issue in their divorce.

- At the 1981 wedding of the Prince of Wales and Lady Diana Spencer, their 2,500 guests drank 1,560 bottles (130 cases) of Bollinger RD champagne.

- It was the only alcohol Marilyn Monroe would touch.

- In 1961, Madame Lily Bollinger, one of champagne's grandes dames, was asked by London's *Daily Mail* when she thought champagne was appropriate. She replied, "I only drink champagne when I'm happy and when I'm sad. Sometimes, I drink it when I'm alone. When I have company, I consider it obligatory. I trifle with it if I'm not hungry and drink it when I am. Otherwise, I never touch it—unless I'm thirsty."

Chocoholics Unite!

Hot chocolate was a well-kept secret of the Spanish royal house for about one hundred years until **Queen Maria Theresa** of Spain introduced the drink to her husband, King Louis XIV of France. He soon appointed a royal chocolate maker, and the delicious drink spread quickly throughout France and then to England.

Both the English and the French regarded chocolate as an aphrodisiac, but reacted differently to this belief. The French drank chocolate freely, but worried about drinking coffee because doctors believed it caused impotence. The English, unworried about coffee, were concerned about the effects of chocolate on women's chastity—men's chastity was not considered nearly as important.

By the end of the eighteenth century, chocolate was no longer considered dangerous to female virtue and was widely drunk all over Europe. During the Enlightenment, ladies of rank and fashion in France would hold salons, where intellectuals would discuss the burning questions of the day while sipping hot chocolate. It wasn't until the nineteenth century that chocolate was pressed into blocks. Here we offer a spirited chocolate drink.

Sue Riding High

1½ ounces dark rum

½ ounce dark crème de cacao

2 ounces hot chocolate, cooled to room temperature

1 teaspoon heavy cream, whipped

In a shaker half-filled with ice cubes, combine the rum, crème de cacao, and hot chocolate. Shake well. Strain into a cocktail glass and top with whipped cream. Serves 1.

Fascinating Feminine Food Facts

- Queen Elizabeth became such an extraordinary devotee of vanilla, that in her later years she allegedly only consumed food and drink enlivened with its flavor.

- In the Gold Rush days of the Wild West, ladies of the night would use half an orange (fruit removed) as a diaphragm.

- The tallest cake in the world, consisting of 100 tiers, was 101 feet, 2½ inches high and was created by Beth Cornell and a team of helpers at the Shiwassee County Fairgrounds in Michigan in August 1990.

- The Aztec word for avocado, ahuacatl, means testicle and Aztec virgins were not allowed outside during avocado harvesting. History doesn't record whether they were allowed to eat them.

- Henry VIII established a cooking school in England to teach his many wives the art of food preparation. While none of the women lasted long, the school has—it is still in existence.

- Cleopatra is said to have bathed in asses' milk, Mary, Queen of Scots in wine (red or white wasn't specified), and novelist George Sand preferred cow's milk (3 quarts) and honey (3 pounds).

Southern Hospitality, Wild Woman Style

In 1863, **Celia** and **Winnie Mae Murphree** were babysitting in Blountsville, Alabama, when three Union soldiers stormed in demanding medical supplies and fresh horses. The soldiers took over the house and demanded to be served mint juleps. Celia and Winnie Mae dutifully prepared the drinks but mixed in a powerful sedative. The Yankees loved the drinks, ordered another round, and after quaffing the second, promptly passed out. The sisters then confiscated the men's weapons and turned them over to the Confederates.

Actually, without knowing it, Celia and Winnie Mae were following a long tradition. Juleps, which are nothing more than sweet-tasting liquids, were used as early as the seventeenth century by pharmacists to disguise the taste of unpleasant medicine. *The Bartender's Bible* speculates that mint juleps were probably originally concocted to disguise the rough taste of whiskey before Kentucky perfected a smooth bourbon.

Mint juleps are traditionally served the first Saturday in May, at the start of the Kentucky Derby. But if you aren't a traditionalist, feel free to imbibe anytime you're in a Scarlett O'Hara mood.

Mint Julep

6 sprigs fresh mint
1 teaspoon superfine sugar

Crushed ice

3 ounces bourbon

Lightly combine 4 of the mint sprigs with the sugar and a few drops of water in the bottom of a high-ball glass. Fill the glass almost to the top with crushed ice. Add the bourbon. Garnish with the remaining 2 mint sprigs and some short straws. Serves 1.

Women on Diets

"[I]f one doesn't have a character like Abraham Lincoln or Joan of Arc, a diet simply disintegrates into eating exactly what you want to eat, but with a bad conscience."

—Maria Augusta Trapp

"I never worry about diets. The only carrots that interest me are the number you get in a diamond."

—Mae West

"Give me a dozen heartbreaks…if you think it would help me lose one pound."

—Colette

"What you eat standing up doesn't count."

—Beth Barnes

"Food is an important part of a balanced diet."

—Fran Lebowitz

"Never eat more than you can lift."

—Miss Piggy

The Coffee Connection

According to Charles Panati in *Extraordinary Origins of Everyday Things,* we have a woman to thank for starting the commercial coffee craze in this country. "In 1907, Mrs. Melitta Bentz of Germany began experimenting with different materials to place between the two chambers of the coffeepot then in use, to prevent grounds from coming through into the drink. She finally hit upon a near-perfect kind of heavy-duty, porous paper in 1908 when she cut a disc from a desk ink blotter, and the Melitta filter system was on its way toward commercial development."

We've named the following drink after Mrs. Melitta; it's a lower-calorie version of another female-associated drink called, for reasons unknown to us, Catherine of Sheridan Square.

Melitta's Madness

1½ ounces dark rum

½ ounce Tia Maria

4 ounces cold coffee

1 ounce nonfat milk

Crushed ice

Fill an Irish coffee glass with crushed ice. Add to it all of the ingredients and stir well. Serves 1.

Irish Coffee

4 ounces hot coffee

1 teaspoon granulated sugar

2 ounces Irish whiskey

2 ounces heavy cream

Pour the coffee into an Irish coffee glass. Add the sugar and stir to dissolve it. Add the whisky and stir. Pour the cream carefully over the back of a teaspoon so that it floats on top of the drink. Serves 1.

Sweeter Than Wine?

In Greek and Roman times, women were not permitted to drink—except for a sweet wine made from raisins, called *passum*. Some men took the injunction quite seriously. Historians report that in the second century B.C., husbands were known to murder their wives if they were discovered sneaking down to the wine cellar for a drop. By the first century A.D., such strictures were lifted, at least for the likes of Livia Augusta, the wife of the emperor Augustus. She credited her long life (86 years) to wine drinking.

– Bibliography –

Ackerman, Diane. *A Natural History of the Senses*. Vintage, 1990.

Anderson, Burton. *Treasures of the Italian Table: Italy's Celebrated Foods and the Artisans Who Make Them*. Morrow, 1994.

Aurandt, Paul. *More of Paul Harvey's Rest of the Story*. Bantam, 1980.

Aylward, Jim. *Things No One Ever Tells You*. Warner, 1980.

Ayres, B. Drummond Jr. "Senate Denounces Talmadge, 81 to 15, Over His Finances." *New York Times*, October 12, 1979, A1.

Bartlett, John. *Familiar Quotations*. Little, Brown and Company, 1992.

Bates, Marston. *Gluttons and Libertines*. Vintage, 1958.

Benning, Lee Edwards. *The Cook's Tales: Origins of Famous Foods and Recipes*. Globe Pequot Press, 1992.

Betty Crocker's Cookbook. Bantam, 1969, 1987.

Blashfield, Jean. *Hellraisers, Heroines, and Holy Women*. St. Martin's Press, 1981.

Bly, Nellie. *Oprah! Up Close and Down Home*. Zebra Books, 1993.

Boulding, Elise. *The Underside of History, Vol. 1*. SAGE Pub., 1992.

Cambridge Biographical Dictionary, 1989 edition.

Carmichael, Bill. *Incredible Collectors, Weird Antiques, and Odd Hobbies*. Warner, 1973.

Chelminski, Rudolph. *The French at Table*. Morrow, 1985.

Colby, C.B. *The Weirdest People in the World*. Scholastic, 1973.

Croutier, Alev Lytle. *Taking the Waters*. Abbeville, 1992.

Daley, Rosie. *In the Kitchen with Rosie: Oprah's Favorite Recipes*. Knopf, 1994.

The Cook's Room. Davidson, Alan, ed. HarperCollins, 1991.

de la Falaise, Maxime. *Food in Vogue*. Doubleday, 1980.

Dineen, Jacqueline. *Chocolate*. Carolrhoda Books, 1991.

Egerton, March. *Since Eve Ate Apples: Quotations on Feasting, Fasting & Food from the Beginning*. Tsunami Press, 1994.

Encyclopedia Americana, 1993 edition.

Encyclopaedia Brittanica, 1994 edition.

Erim, Kenan. *Aphrodisiacs*. Facts on File, 1986.

Esquivel, Laura. *Like Water for Chocolate*. Doubleday, 1989.

Fisher, M.F.K. *The Art of Eating*. Collier Books, 1990.

Flagg, *Fannie. Fannie Flagg's Original Whistle Stop Cafe Cookbook*. Fawcett Columbine, 1993.

Foster, Nelson, et al. *Chilies to Chocolate*. University of Arizona Press, 1992.

Frazier, Greg and Beverly. *Aphrodisiac Cookery*. Troubadour, 1970.

Gaar, Gillian G. *She's a Rebel: The History of Women in Rock & Roll*. Seal Press, 1992.

Gardner, Robert. *Kitchen Chemistry*. Julian Messner, 1982.

Giblin, James Cross. *From Hand to Mouth*. Crowell, 1987.

A Literary Feast. Golden, Lilly, ed. Atlantic Monthly Press, 1993.

Grant, Michael. *Cleopatra*. Barnes & Noble, 1992.

Griffin, Lynne, et al. *The Book of Women*. Bob Adams, 1992.

Harris, Marvin. *Cows, Pigs, Wars, and Witches*. Vintage, 1974.

——. *The Sacred Cow and the Abominable Pig*. Touchstone, 1985.

Hearst, Patricia. *Every Secret Thing*. Pinnacle, 1982.

James, Peter, and Nick Thorpe. *Ancient Inventions*. Ballantine, 1994.

Jansz, Balasuriya, Heather, et al. *Fire & Spice*. McGraw-Hill, 1989.

Josephus, Flavius. *The Complete Works of Josephus*. Kregel, 1960.

Kasdan, Sara. *Love and Knishes: An Irrepressible Guide to Jewish Cooking.* Vanguard Press, 1956, 1964.

Kelley, Kitty. *Nancy Reagan.* Pocket Star Books, 1991.

Landes, Ruth. *The Ojibwa Woman.* Norton, 1938.

León, Vicki. *Uppity Women of Ancient Times.* Conari, 1995.

Lowell, Ivana et al. *An Appetite for Passion Cookbook.* Miramax, 1995.

Lucaire, Edward. *Celebrity Trivia.* Warner, 1980.

Lukins, Sheila. *All Around the World Cookbook.* Workman, 1994.

MacClancy, Jeremy. *Consuming Culture.* Holt, 1992.

Macksey, Joan, et al. *The Guinness Book of Women's Achievements.* Stein and Day, 1975.

Maggio, Rosalie. *The Beacon Book of Quotations by Women.* Beacon, 1992.

Martin, Ralph. *Golda: The Romantic Years.* Scribner's, 1988.

Martinetz, Dieter, et al. *Poison.* Edition Leipzig, 1987.

Matthews, Peter, et al. *The Guinness Book of Records, 1993.* Bantam, 1993 edition.

McConnell, Brian. *Holy Killers.* Headline Books, 1995.

McConnell, Jane and Burt. *Our First Ladies.* Crowell, 1969.

McFarlan, Donald, ed. *The Guinness Book of Records, 1992.* Facts on File, 1991.

McGee, Harold. On Food and Cooking. Collier/Macmillan, 1984.

McGlashan, C.F. *History of the Donner Party.* Stanford University Press, 1940.

McGrady, Mike. *Out of Bondage.* Lyle Stuart, 1986.

McKenny, Margaret. *The Savory Wild Mushroom.* University of Washington Press, 1962.

Meir, Menahem. *My Mother Golda Meir.* Arbor Books, 1983.

Meldrum, Douglas. *The Night 2000 Men Came to Dinner.* Scribner's, 1994.

Merriam Webster's Encyclopedia of Literature. Merriam-Webster, 1995.

Mills, Jane. Womanwords. Holt, 1989.

Montoya-Welsh, Sharon, et al. *Oyster Cookery*. Shoalwater Kitchen, 1994.

Morland, Nigel. *That Nice Miss Smith*. St. Martin's Press, 1988.

Morris, Terry. *Shalom Golda*. Hawthorne, 1971.

Myers, Robert. *Celebrations*. Doubleday, 1972.

The National Council of Negro Women. *Celebrating Our Mothers' Kitchens*. Tradery, 1994.

Norwood Pratt, James. *Tea Lover's Treasury*. Cole, 1982.

O'Neill, Lois. *The Women's Book of World Records and Achievements*. Anchor Books, 1979.

Panati, Charles. *Extraordinary Origins of Everyday Things*. Harper & Row, 1987.

———. *Panati's Parade of Fads, Follies, and Manias*. Harper Perennial, 1991.

Piercy, Caroline. *The Shaker Cookbook*. Weathervane Books, 1986.

Pliny the Elder. *Natural History*. Loeb Classical Library series, Harvard University Press, 1983.

Reader's Digest. *Who's Who in the Bible*. Reader's Digest, 1994.

Regan, Gary. *The Bartender's Bible*. HarperCollins, 1991.

Revel, Jean-Francois. *Culture and Cuisine: A Journey Through the History of Food*. Translated from the French by Helen R. Lane. Doubleday, 1979.

Rodriguez-Hunter, Suzanne. *Found Meals of the Lost Generation: Recipes and Anecdotes from 1920s Paris*. Faber and Faber, 1994.

Ritchie, Caron. *Food in Civilization*. Beauford Books, 1981.

Rivera, Guadalupe and Marie-Pierre Colle., *Frida's Fiestas: Recipes and Reminiscences of Life with Frida Kahlo*. Clarkson Potter, 1994.

Russo, Julee. *Great Good Food: Luscious Lower-Fat Cooking*. Crown, 1993.

Salmonson, Jessica. *The Encyclopedia of Amazons*. Doubleday, 1991.

Sandburg, Carl. *Abraham Lincoln*. Harcourt Brace, 1926.

Schivelbusch, Wolfgang. *Tastes of Paradise*. Vintage, 1992.

Sheraton, Mimi. "Mimi Sheraton Picks the Top 10 Women Cooks of 1996," in: *New Woman,* January, 1996.

Slater, Robert. *Golda, the Uncrowned Queen of Israel.* Jonathon David Publishers, 1981.

Smallzried, Kathleen Ann. *The Everlasting Pleasure: Influences on America's Kitchens, Cooks, and Cookery from 1565 to the Year 2000.* Appleton-Century-Crofts, 1956.

Smith, Bernie. *The Joy of Trivia.* Brooke House, 1976.

Smith Booth, Sally. *Hung, Strung and Potted.* Clarkson Potter, 1971.

Stevens, Peter. *The Mayflower Murderer & Other Forgotten Firsts in American History.* Morrow, 1993.

St. John, Dick and Sandy, with Des Barres, Pamela. *The Rock & Roll Cookbook: Favorite Recipes from the Chart Toppers, Hit Makers and Legends of Rock & Roll.* General Publishing Group, 1993.

Tannahill, Reay. *Food in History.* Penguin, 1973; Crown, 1989.

Taylor, Elizabeth. *Elizabeth Takes Off.* Putnam, 1987.

Tibol, Raquel. *Frida Kahlo. An Open Life.* Translated by Elinor Randall. University of New Mexico Press, 1993.

Tierney, Patrick. *The Highest Altar.* Penguin, 1989.

Toklas, Alice B. *The Alice B. Toklas Cookbook.* Harper & Row, 1954, 1984.

Tolbert, Frank. *A Bowl of Red.* Doubleday, 1966.

Toussant-Samat, Maguelonne. *History of Food.* Blackwell, 1987.

Trager, James. *The Food Chronology.* Holt, 1995.

——. *The Women's Chronology.* Holt, 1994.

Tropp, Barbara. *China Moon Cookbook.* Workman, 1992.

Visser, Margaret. *Much Depends on Dinner.* Grove Press, 1986.

Wallenchinsky, David, et al. *The Book of Lists.* Bantam, 1978.

——. *The People's Almanac.* Doubleday, 1975.

_____. *The People's Almanac #2*. Bantam, 1978.

Waterhouse, Debra. *Why Women Need Chocolate: What You Crave to Look and Feel Great*. Hyperion, 1995.

West, J.B. *Upstairs at the White House*. Warner, 1973.

Williams, Jacqueline. *Wagon Wheel Kitchens*. University Press of Kansas, 1993.

Williams, Lena. "Gracious Guidance for Real People," in: *New York Times*, Dec 13, 1995.

de Witt, Karen. "Senator's Ex-Wife Goes It Alone," in: *New York Times*, May 24, 1978, C1.

de Witt, Karen. "Talmadge's Former Wife Enters Contest for a Seat in the House," in: *New York Times*, May 11, 1978.

World Almanac, editors of. *The World Almanac Book of the Strange*. New American Library, 1977.

World Book, 1992 edition.

Worth, Fred L. *The Complete Unabridged Super Trivia Encyclopedia*. Warner, 1977.

Young, Hugo. *Iron Lady: Biography of Margaret Thatcher*. Farrar Straus & Giroux, 1989.

- Index -

– Permissions –

We give thanks for permission to excerpt from the following works:

Uppity Women of Ancient Times by Vicki León. Copyright © 1995 by Vicki León. Reprinted by permission of Conari Press.

Wild Women: Crusaders, Curmudgeons and Completely Corsetless Ladies in the Otherwise Virtuous Victorian Era by Autumn Stephens. Copyright © 1992 by Autumn Stephens. Reprinted by permission of Conari Press.

Diane Clement at the Tomato by Diane Clement. Copyright © 1995 by Diane Clement. Reprinted by permission of Raincoast Books.

Betty Crocker's Cookbook: New and Revised. Copyright © 1987 by General Mills. Reprinted by permission of General Mills.

From *Fannie Flagg's Original Whistle Stop Cafe Cookbook* by Fannie Flagg. Copyright © 1993 by Fannie Flagg. Reprinted by permission of Ballantine Books, a Division of Random House Inc.

From *Great Good Food* by Julee Russo. Copyright © 1993 by Julee Russo. Reprinted by permission of Crown Publishers, Inc.

"Haschich Fudge" from *The Alice B. Toklas Cookbook* by Alice B. Toklas. Copyright © 1954 by Alice B. Toklas. Copyright renewed 1982 by Edward M. Burns. Reprinted by permission of HarperCollins Publishers, Inc.

Excerpts from *The Rock & Roll Cookbook. Favorite Recipes from the Chart Toppers, Hit Makers and Legends of Rock & Roll* by Dick and Sandy St. John. Copyright © 1993 by the National Music Foundation. Reprinted by permission of General publishing Group, Inc.

"Madras Chicken Salad" from *All Around the World Cookbook* by Sheila Lukins. Copyright © 1994 by Sheila Lukins. Reprinted by permission of Workman Publishing Company, Inc. All rights reserved.

Lynette Rohrer

Lynette Rohrer's inspiration came from her Hungarian great-grandmother, who brought her Old World recipes with her to the Midwest. Lynette's special talent for desserts began as a child helping stretch paper-thin pastry for strudel across the dining room table. Her professional culinary career began in Columbus, Ohio making pizza. Lynette trained as a chef at the California Culinary Academy and has since cooked for several world-class restaurants including Chez Panisse, Postrio, Masa's Bizou, and now Star's. Lynette is sharing here for the first time many of the recipes she created for these four-star restaurants.

Nicole Alper

Nicole Alper has lived in Northern California for most of her life. Born to a Parisian mother, Nicole acquired a love of fine food early on, prompting her to study at the prestigious California Culinary Academy where she focused her training in French classical cooking and once had the honor of preparing a special meal for the great Julia Child. Nicole honed her cooking skills in Paris and Provence and is in the planning stages of her own restaurant in San Francisco.

Wild Women Association

In 1992, with the publication of *Wild Women* by Autumn Stephens, Conari Press founded the Wild Women Association. Today there are over 3,000 card-carrying Wild Women in cities throughout the world—and some even meet regularly with their untamed and uproarious sisters in an effort to encourage wildness. The Association's primary purpose is to rediscover and rewrite our wild foresisters back into history. . . . and if there is a wild woman in your family we hope you might help by sending us information for possible inclusion in subsequent volumes of the Wild Women series.

To become a member and to receive the Wild Women Association Newsletter, please mail this page to:

The Wild Women Association
2550 Ninth Street, Suite 101
Berkeley, CA 94710

If you'd like a *Wild Women in the Kitchen* magnet, send a copy of
this page along with $3.00 to the address above.

Let's rewrite history with women in it!

Conari Press, established in 1987, publishes books on topics
ranging from spirituality and women's history to sexuality and
personal growth. Our main goal is to publish quality books
that will make a difference in people's lives—both
how we feel about ourselves and how
we relate to one another.

Our readers are our most important resource, and we
value your input, suggestions, and ideas. We'd love to hear
from you—after all, we are publishing
books for you!

For a complete catalog or to get on our mailing list,
please contact us at:

CONARI PRESS
2550 Ninth Street, Suite 101
Berkeley, California 94710

(800) 685-9595 • Fax (510) 649-7190
e-mail: Conaripub@aol.com